Vertical Lines

II

A Compilation of Sarcasm, Word Play, and Witticisms

Edited By

ANDREW A. FELDER

To readers of **the network**, without whose support and encouragement, this volume would never have been completed.

Published by CREST Publications Group, Fort Worth, Texas

ISBNs
9798885266390 (Print)
9798885266499 (E-book)

www.crestpublicationsgroup.com

COVER DESIGN: SHUMAILA REHMAN
TECHNICAL DIRECTOR: MARIA TARIQ

Vertical Lines II

Note from the editor:

They come from anywhere and everywhere – words of wisdom, insults, funny quotes, word play – just fun and interesting stuff. It was one of our readers who (while submitting a few lines for us to use in **the network**) suggested compiling them into a book – and "Viola!" [the immortal word of Kelly Bundy on the television sitcom *Married With Children*], there it was! And here it is – timeless!

Two years later, this is Book II. And, as long as you keep enjoying them, we'll keep them coming.

People are making end-of-the-world jokes like there's no tomorrow.

The problem isn't that obesity runs in your family. It's that no one runs in your family.

I asked my husband if I was the only one he had ever slept with. He said yes, all the others were nines or tens.

4 out of 3 people struggle with math.

Your future depends on your dreams. Don't waste any time; go to bed now.

Your kid may be an honor student but you're still an idiot!

'God is dead.' – Nietzsche. 'Nietzsche is dead.' - God

"I am" is reportedly the shortest sentence in the English language. Could it be that "I do" is the longest sentence?

"I am" is supposedly the shortest sentence in the English language. Could it be that "I do" is the longest sentence?

"I have a split personality," said Tom, being Frank.

The ideal man doesn't smoke, doesn't drink, doesn't do drugs, doesn't swear, doesn't get angry, doesn't exist.

"Tired" isn't even a temporary state for me anymore. It's more like a part of my personality at this point.

"With all due respect" is a polite way of saying, "Listen here, you little shit."

My husband and I decided that we don't want to have children. We'll be telling them tonight.

A cold seat in a public restroom is unpleasant. A warm seat in a public restroom is worse.

"Be careful about reading health books. You may die of a misprint." (Mark Twain)

I'm single by choice. Unfortunately, it's not my choice.

"By all means, marry. If you get a good wife, you'll become happy; if you get a bad one, you'll become a philosopher." (Socrates)

"I have a split personality," said Tom, being Frank.

"I have never hated a man enough to give his diamonds back." (Zsa Zsa Gabor)

A blind man walked into a bar... and a table... and a chair...

"I never drink water because of the disgusting things that fish do in it." (W. C. Fields)

Just because I don't care doesn't mean I'm not listening.

A private tutor is a person who doesn't fart in public

"Last week, I stated this woman was the ugliest woman I had ever seen. I have since been visited by her sister, and now wish to withdraw that statement." (Mark Twain)

"Learning to dislike children at an early age saves a lot of expense and aggravation later in life." (Ed Byrne)

"Oh, when I was a kid in show business, I was poor. I used to go to orgies to eat the grapes." (Rodney Dangerfield)

It was all so different zent before everything changed.

"She was an open book. He was illiterate."
(Maya Angelou)

"Sometimes, when I look at my children, I say
to myself, 'Lillian, you should have remained
a virgin.'" (Lillian Carter, mother of Jimmy
Carter)

"We didn't inherit this planet from our
ancestors, we borrowed it from our children
(Lakota Sioux saying)

I'm writing a book about hurricanes and
tornados... It's only a draft at the moment.

I am in shape. Round is a shape.

Sometimes I wake up grumpy; other times I
let him sleep.

1 in 5 people in the world are Chinese. There
are 5 people in my family, so it must be one
of them. It's either my mom or my dad. Or my
older brother Steve. Or my younger brother
Ho-Cha-Chu. But I think it's Steve.

3 Religious truths: Jews do not recognize
Jesus as the Messiah. Protestants do not
recognize the Pope as the leader of the
Christian faith. Baptists do not recognize
each other in the liquor store or at Hooters.

I'm changing my name to 'Benefits' on Facebook. Next time someone adds me, it will say, 'You are now friends with Benefits.'

Before was was was was, was was is.

"I was married by a judge. I should have asked for a jury." (Groucho Marx)

42 percent of all statistics are made up! (Including this one.)

The seven ages of man: spills, drills, thrills, bills, ills, pills, and wills.

I have an inferiority complex, but it's not a very good one.

Stupidity is not a crime, so you're free to go.

6:30 is the best time on a clock, hands down.

A beggar walked up to a well-dressed woman shopping on Rodeo Drive and said, "I haven't eaten anything in four days." She looked at him and said, "God, I wish I had your willpower."

Some people hear voices. Some see invisible people. Others have no imagination whatsoever.

A blonde heard that accidents happen close to home ... so she moved.

Sometimes I wish life had subtitles.

It's hard to explain puns to kleptomaniacs. They're always taking things... literally.

A cartoonist was found dead in his home. Details are sketchy.

"I like a woman with a head on her shoulders. I hate necks." (Steve Martin)

A child came home from his first day at school. His mother asked, 'What did you learn today?" The kid replied, "Not enough. They want me to come back tomorrow."

"I looked up my family tree and found three dogs using it." (Rodney Dangerfield)

Some people just need a sympathetic pat on the head...with a hammer.

A closed mouth gathers no foot.

What do you call a boomerang that doesn't come back? A stick.

Don't irritate old people. The older they get, the less "Life in prison" is a deterrent.

I really don't mind getting older, but my body is taking it badly.

It turns out that being an adult now is mostly just googling how to do stuff.

The dinner I was cooking for my family was going to be a surprise, but the fire trucks ruined it.

I miss the 90's when bread was still good for you and no one knew what kale was.

Marriage is full of surprises but it's mostly just asking each other, "Do you have to do that right now?"

Nurse: "We need a stool sample and a urine sample." Husband to wife: "What did she say?" Wife to husband: "They want your underwear."

The doctor refused to write me a prescription for Viagra. He said it would be like putting a new flagpole on a condemned building.

Do you ever get up in the morning, look in the mirror and think "That can't be right."

Irony — the opposite of wrinkly.

As I watch this new generation try to rewrite our history, one thing I'm sure of....it will be misspelled and have no punctuation.

Good men are found in every corner of the Earth. Unfortunately, the Earth is round.

Confuse your doctor by putting on rubber gloves at the same time he does.

A conclusion is the part where you got tired of thinking.

Some people think prison is one word...but to robbers it's a whole sentence.

The farther away the future is, the better it looks.

A cop accidentally arrested a judge who was dressed like a convict for a costume party. He learned to never book a judge by their cover.

The first computer dates back to Adam and Eve. It was an Apple with limited memory— just one byte. And then everything crashed.

The first novel ever written on a typewriter was *Tom Sawyer.*

Daffynition: Shin—a device for finding furniture in the dark.

The first rule of holes: if you're in one, stop digging.

A couple came upon a wishing well. The husband leaned over, made a wish, and threw in a penny. The wife decided to make a wish, too. But she leaned over too much, fell into the well, and drowned. The husband was stunned for a while but then smiled and thought to himself, 'It really works!'

A couple years ago my therapist told me I had problems letting go of the past.

A courtroom artist was arrested today for an unknown reason. Details are sketchy.

Refusing to go to the gym is a form of resistance training.

A day for firm decisions! Or is it?

A day without sunshine is like ... a day in Seattle.

You're not fat; you're just easier to see.

Kids in the backseat cause accidents.
Accidents in the backseat cause kids.

What do you call a woman who knows where her husband is every night? A widow.

A doctor told a woman she could no longer touch anything alcoholic. So she got a divorce.

A cop knocked on my door and told me that my dogs were chasing people on bikes. I told him that couldn't be because my dogs don't even own bikes.

A Freudian slip is when you say one thing and mean your mother.

A friend is someone who will help you move. A good friend is someone who will help you move a dead body.

I'm glad to see you're not letting your education get in the way of your ignorance.

A graduation ceremony is an event where the commencement speaker tells thousands of students dressed in identical caps and gowns that 'individuality' is the key to success.

A guy with a stutter died in prison before he could finish his sentence.

A husband is someone who takes out the trash and gives the impression he just cleaned the whole house.

A liberal is a conservative who's been arrested. A conservative is a liberal who's been mugged.

People who take care of chickens are literally chicken tenders.

A little boy killed a butterfly. His father said, "No butter for one week." Then the little boy killed a honeybee, and his father said, "No honey for one week." Then his mom killed a cockroach, and the little boy turned to his father and said, "Are you going to tell her, or should I?"

What do you call a magic owl? Whooo-dini.

A man put an 'ad' in the classifieds: 'Wife wanted." Next day he received a hundred letters. They all said the same thing: "You can have mine."

Never attribute to malice what can be adequately explained by stupidity.

Why do bees hum? Because they don't remember the lyrics.

A man without a woman is like a fish without a bicycle.

A met a really hot girl who was half Japanese and half Philippino. I think I ruined it by calling her Jalapeco.

A Mexican magician told the audience that he would disappear on the count of three. He said, "Uno, dos..." and poof! He disappeared without a tres.

A New Year's resolution is something that goes in one year and out the other.

A pat on the back is only a few centimeters from a kick in the butt.

Electricians have to strip to make ends meet.

Elephants are the only animals that can't jump.

A plateau is the highest form of flattery.

Young bike riders pick a destination and go. Old bike riders pick a direction and go.

A psychiatrist is a person who will give you expensive answers that your spouse will give you for free.

A recent study has found that women who carry a little extra weight live longer than the men who mention it.

A secret is something which is told to one person at a time.

People used to laugh at me when I'd say, "I want to be a comedian." Well, nobody's laughing now.

What do you call a mac 'n' cheese that gets all up in your face? Too close for comfort food!

A shoutout to everyone who can still remember their childhood phone number but can't remember the password they created yesterday. You are my people!

A study of economics usually reveals that the best time to buy anything was last year.

A teacher asked a student, "Are you ignorant or just apathetic?" The kid answered, "I don't know, and I don't care."

I told my girlfriend she drew her eyebrows too high. She seemed surprised.

A transvestite is a guy who likes to eat, drink and be Mary!

A vegan said to me, "People who sell meat are gross!" I said, "People who sell fruits and vegetables are grocer."

Our mountains aren't just funny, they're hill areas.

Out of my mind. Back in five minutes.

A wise man once said... nothing... he only listened.

A woman has the last word in any argument. Anything a man says after that is the beginning of a new argument.

A woman never wakes up her second baby just to see it smile.

What do you call a factory that makes OK products? A satisfactory.

A woman with a past is interesting to men. They hope history will repeat itself.

The women's work that is never done is the stuff she asked her husband to do.

About a month before he died, my uncle had his back covered in lard. After that, he went downhill fast.

Adult: Someone who has stopped growing at both ends and now grows in the middle.

According to a new survey, women say they feel more comfortable undressing in front of men than they do undressing in front of other women. They say that women are too judgmental, while men, of course, are just grateful.

Don't argue with an idiot. He will drag you down to his level and beat you with experience.

What do you call a dog magician? A labracadabrador.

According to most studies, people's number one fear is public speaking. Number two is death. Death is number two—does that sound right? That means to the average person, if you go to a funeral, you're better off in the casket than doing the eulogy.

Age 60 might be the new 40, but 9 PM is the new midnight.

Then there was a man who said, "I never knew what real happiness was until I got married… and then it was too late."

Funny, I don't remember being absent minded.

All I ask is a chance to prove money can't make me happy.

If ignorance is bliss, you must be the happiest person on earth.

All power corrupts. Absolute power is pretty neat, though.

They tell you that you'll lose your mind when you grow older. What they don't tell you is that you won't miss it very much.

They told me I had type-A blood, but it was a typo.

What do you call a dinosaur with an extensive vocabulary? A thesaurus.

All reports are in—life is now officially unfair.

Allow me to introduce my selves.

Veni, Vedi, Visa: I came, I saw, I did a little shopping.

Although I have to repeat myself several times for my children to listen, I take great comfort knowing that one day nothing will annoy them more than me repeating myself.

Always give 100% at work: 12% Monday, 23% Tuesday, 40% Wednesday, 20% Thursday, 5% Friday.

When a woman says, "We need to talk," she really means you need to listen.

When confronted by a difficult problem, you can solve it more easily by reducing it to the question, "How would the Lone Ranger handle this?"

My wife is on a tropical fruit diet, the house is full of the stuff! It's enough to make a mango crazy.

When cheese gets its picture taken, what does it say?

My wife just found out I replaced our bed with a trampoline. She hit the ceiling!

Always remember that you are unique...just like everyone else.

Alzheimer's isn't so bad. At least you get to meet new people every day.

When everything is coming your way —
you're in the wrong lane.

Americans on the average eat 18 acres of
pizza every day.

Among the things that are so simple even a
child can operate them are parents.

An amnesiac walks into a bar. He goes up to a
beautiful blonde and says, "So, do I come
here often?"

What do you call a deer with no eyes? No
eye deer.

When I ask you for directions, please don't
use words like 'east'.

An ant can lift 50 times its own weight, can
pull 30 times its own weight and always fails
over on its right side when intoxicated.

An archaeologist is the best husband a
woman can have; the older she gets the more
interested he is in her.

(An) opinion without 3.14159 is just an onion.

An optimist believes that we live in the best world. A pessimist is afraid that that might be true.

An ostrich's eye is bigger than its brain.

I can't remember if I've forgotten that before.

Anger is a feeling that makes your mouth work faster than your mind.

When I found out that my toaster wasn't waterproof, I was shocked.

Animal testing is a terrible idea. They get all nervous and give the wrong answers.

Any married person should forget their mistakes. No use two people remembering the same thing.

Anyone who wanted to sell fish had to get permission from grandpa. He was known as the cod father.

Some people didn't fall from the stupid tree, they were dragged through the entire dumbass forest!

When I get naked in the bathroom, the shower usually gets turned on.

Anything free is worth what you pay for it.

Anytime four New Yorkers get into a cab together without arguing, a bank robbery has just taken place.

Apparently, I snore so loudly that it scares everyone in the car I'm driving.

I danced like no one was watching. My court date is pending.

What do you call a clown who's in jail? A silicon.

Apparently, saying, 'Wow, you've grown since I last saw you,' isn't socially acceptable when said to adults.

Arguing with a woman is like buying a lottery ticket. You know you're not going to win, but you're sure as hell going to try.

Artificial intelligence is no match for natural stupidity.

My girlfriend said she was leaving me because I kept pretending to be a Transformer. I said, "No, wait! I can change."

What do you call a dancing lamb? A baaaaaa-llerina.

As I get older and remember all the people I've lost along the way, I think to myself maybe a career as a tour guide wasn't for me.

As I watched the dog chasing his tail I thought, 'Dogs are easily amused.' I smiled… and then I realized I was watching the dog chasing his tail.

I did some financial planning, and it looks like I can retire at 62 and live comfortably for eleven minutes.

When I have a headache, I take two aspirins and keep away from children – just like it says on the bottle.

As soon as you lose the ability to control your digestive system, it's all over…

Don't tell me I don't know the difference between right and wrong. Wrong is the fun one.

Don't trust atoms, they make up everything.

At my funeral, take the bouquet off my coffin and throw it into the crowd to see who's next.

When I say, 'The other day,' I could be referring to any time between yesterday and 15 years ago.

At my job, I have 500 people under me. I'm a security guard at a cemetery.

Some of us learn from the mistakes of others; the rest of us have to be the others.

At the feast of ego, everyone leaves hungry.

When I walk into a spider web, I demolish his home and misplace his dinner... yet I still feel like the victim.

What do you call a bear with no teeth? A gummy bear.

At what age is it appropriate to tell my dog that he's adopted?

Some people are alive only because it's against the law to kill them.

At work, the authority of a person is inversely proportional to the number of pens that person is carrying.

Atheism is a non-prophet organization.

What do you call a Russian procrastinator? Putinitoff.

When I was a kid, I wanted to be older. This crap is not what I expected.

Avoid arguments about the toilet seat...use the sink.

How is a government worker like a shotgun with a broken firing pin? It won't work, and you can't fire it.

What did 50 Cent do when he got hungry? 58

I like the way your medication thinks.

I like to hold hands at the movies... which always seems to startle strangers.

I like to show my girlfriend who's boss in our house by holding a mirror up to her face.

Aww, it's so cute when you try to talk about things you don't understand.

Bachelors know more about women than married men; if they didn't, they'd be married too. (H. L. Mencken)

Banging your head against a wall burns 150 calories an hour.

Be careful of your thoughts. They may become words at any moment.

I like you. You remind me of when I was young and stupid.

I lost my job at the bank on my very first day. A woman asked me to check her balance, so I pushed her over.

Be useless, so nobody can use you.

Beer nuts for sale — $1.25 per bag. Deer nuts are under a buck.

I got gas for $1.39 today. Unfortunately, it was at Taco Bell.

Some people are like Slinkies ... not really good for anything, but you can't help smiling when you see one tumble down the stairs.

Before marriage, a man yearns for the woman he loves. After marriage, the "y" becomes silent.

I didn't think orthopedic shoes would help, but I stand corrected.

When I was young, I felt like a male trapped in a female's body. Then I was born.

I don't find it hard to meet expenses. They're everywhere.

Before you criticize someone, walk a mile in their shoes. That way, when you *do* criticize them, you're a mile away and you have their shoes.

What do you call an Alabama farmer with a sheep under each arm? A pimp.

If I make you breakfast in bed, a simple "thank you" is all I need. Not all this "how did you get in my house?!" business.

When life gives you melons, you might be dyslexic.

When Miley Cyrus gets naked & licks a hammer it's 'art" & "music.' But when I do it, I'm 'drunk' and 'have to leave the hardware store.'

If I want your opinion, I'll ask you to fill out the necessary forms.

Behind every angry woman is a man who has absolutely no idea what he did wrong.

Build a man a fire and he'll be warm for a day.
Set a man on fire and he'll be warm for the
rest of his life.

By the time you learn the rules of life, you're
too old to play the game.

Camping — where you spend a small fortune
to live like a homeless person.

Can a kangaroo jump higher than the Empire
State Building? Of course. The Empire State
Building can't jump.

You come from dust. You will return to dust.
That's why I don't dust. It could be someone I
know.

Can I have your picture so I can show Santa
what I want for Christmas?

Canadians say "sorry" so much that a law was
passed in 2009 declaring that an apology can't
be used as evidence of an admission of guilt.

I'm so miserable without you, it's almost like
you're still here.

Change is inevitable, except from a vending
machine.

Bureaucrats cut red tape...lengthwise.

Butterflies taste with their feet.

Chaos, panic, and disorder. My work here is done.

You have the capacity to learn from your mistakes, and you will learn a lot today.

Childhood is like being drunk. Everyone remembers what you did, except you.

Clinging on to past and living is like driving forward while watching the rear-view mirror.

Coca-Cola was originally green.

Comedy is tragedy plus time.

Life is all about perspective. The sinking of the Titanic was a miracle to the lobsters in the ship's kitchen.

If you do not say it, they can't repeat it.

Communist jokes aren't funny unless everyone gets them.

You have the right to remain silent because whatever you say will probably be stupid anyway.

You never really learn to swear until you learn to drive.

Only argue with your wife when she's not around.

Conception occurs more often in December than any other month.

Women should not have children after 35 — 35 children are enough!

Confucius says, 'Man who runs behind car will get exhausted, but man who runs in front of car will get tired.'

Courage is knowing it might hurt and doing it anyway. Stupidity is exactly the same thing, and that's why life is hard.

Being a hypochondriac is going to save my life one of these days.

If I wanted to hear from an asshole, I'd fart.

Being an adult is just walking around wondering what you're forgetting.

She: "Nothing rhymes with orange." He: "No it doesn't."

She: "What do you do in your spare time?" He: "I stalk." She: "Really? I enjoy walks in the park or going to the movies with my friends." He: "I know."

Shoutout to the person who created the word 'plethora.' It means a lot.

Birthdays are good for you. Statistics show that the people who have the most live the longest!

Women who seek to be equal to men lack ambition.

Blunt pencils are really pointless.

If I've learned anything in life, it's that not enough people are at a loss for words.

You have to stay in shape. My grandmother started walking five miles a day when she was 60. She's 97 today and we have no idea where she is.

Life is a comedy for those who think, but a tragedy for those who feel.

If you don't care where you are, then you aren't lost.

Brains are wonderful. I wish everyone had one.

A cow stumbled into pot field. The steaks have never been higher.

Cows have hooves because they lactose.

Crime doesn't pay. Does that mean that my job is a crime?

When a man says, "I'm fine," he actually means it. When a woman says, "I don't want anything for Valentine's Day," it's the same as her saying 'I'm fine.'

You know that tingly little feeling you get when you like someone? That's your common sense leaving your body.

Women will drive miles out of their way to avoid the possibility of getting lost using a shortcut.

Work hard and save your money and when you are old you will be able to buy the things only the young can enjoy.

Crushing pop cans is soda pressing.

When a newly married couple smiles, everyone knows why. When a ten-year married couple smiles, everyone wonders why.

Daffynition: Consciousness—that annoying time between naps.

Dating a single mother is like continuing from somebody else's saved game.

Day 12 without chocolate — lost hearing in my left eye.

Why did Noah include termites on the ark?

You get only spoiled milk from a pampered cow.

What do you call a seagull that flies over the bay? A bagel.

It's always darkest before dawn. So, if you're going to steal your neighbor's newspaper, that's the time to do it.

You know what I did before I married? Anything I wanted to.

It's hard to make a comeback when you haven't been anywhere.

You can't get on the same page with someone who has a different book.

You can't kill yourself by holding your breath.

Men don't realize that if we're sleeping with them on the first date, we're probably not interested in seeing them again either.

Middle age is when work is a lot less fun, and fun is a lot more work.

Misspell one word and the whole text is urined.

Moms have Mother's Day, Dads have Father's Day. What do single guys have? Palm Sunday.

Daffynition: Retired: I was tired yesterday and I'm tired again today.

Depression is merely anger without enthusiasm.

Thieves broke into my house and stole everything except my soap, shower gel, towels, and deodorant. Dirty bastards!

Despite the high cost of living, it remains popular.

Did you ever notice when you blow in a dog's face, he gets mad at you? But when you take him in a car, he sticks his head out the window.

Did you hear about the Italian chef who died? He pasta way. We cannoli do so much. His legacy will become a pizza history. He ran out of thyme.

Never miss an opportunity to sit down and shut up.

Cleaning mirrors is a job I could really see myself doing.

Don't underestimate me! That's my mother's job.

She: "Do you play any sports?" He: "I run away from my feelings."

She: "Every time I get in the shower, I think of you." He: "Is that because you wish I were there with you?" She: "No, it's because the French word for shower is 'douche'."

I always wanted to be somebody, but now I realize I should have been more specific.

What do you call a snobby criminal walking down the steps? A condescending con descending!

If it wasn't for the last minute, nothing would get done.

If it's true that we are here to help others, then what exactly are the others here for?

My body is a temple – ancient and crumbling (and probably cursed or haunted).

You know when you're getting older by remembering the past embarrassment of not zipping up your fly but now hoping you remember when to unzip.

We are born naked, wet, and hungry. Then things get worse.

Don't worry, it only seems kinky the first time.

It's been raining for 3 days without stopping. My wife is so depressed. She is standing and staring through the window. If the rain doesn't stop tomorrow, I'll have to let her in.

I'm friends with 25 letters of the alphabet. I don't know Y.

I'm glad I know sign language; it's pretty handy.

Cleaning your house while your kids are still growing is like clearing the drive before it has stopped snowing.

Clinging on to past and living is like driving forward while watching the rear-view mirror.

I am an agent of Satan, but my duties are largely ceremonial.

You know you're ugly when it comes to a group picture, and they hand you the camera.

I saw an ad for burial plots and thought to myself: that's the last thing I need.

Captain Hook died from jock itch.

Dolphins are so smart that within a few weeks of captivity, they can train people to stand on the very edge of the pool and throw them fish.

When one door closes and another one opens, you are probably in prison.

Don't take life too seriously. You'll never get out of it alive.

You know what I saw today? Everything I looked at.

Do not walk behind me, for I may not lead. Do not walk ahead of me, for I may not follow. Do not walk beside me, either. Just leave me the hell alone.

Do you know the punishment for bigamy? Two mothers-in-law.

What do you call a three-foot-tall aardvark? A yardvark.

It's better to let someone think you're an idiot than to open your mouth and prove it.

It's easier to remember your age if you don't change it every year.

We come to love not by finding a perfect person... but by learning to see an imperfect person perfectly.

When someone asks what I did over the weekend, I squint and ask, "Why? What did you hear?"

Doctor: "Your body has run out of magnesium." Me: "OMG!"

You know your children are growing up when they stop asking you where they came from and refuse to tell you where they're going.

Dogs can't operate MRI scanners, but Catscan.

Doesn't expecting the unexpected make the unexpected become the expected?

We need to look at how the world really works, not just accept the way we are told it works.

I bought the world's worst thesaurus yesterday. Not only is it terrible, it's also terrible.

When someone says, "Do you want my opinion?" - it's always a negative one.

Drink coffee! Do stupid things faster with more energy!

During my interview today, I poured some water into a cup, and it overflowed a little bit. "Nervous?" asked the interviewer. I replied, "No. I just always give 110%."

Each king in a deck of playing cards represents a great king from history: Spades -

King David, Hearts -Charlemagne, Clubs -
Alexander the Great, Diamonds - Julius
Caesar.

I like birthdays but too many can kill you.

Dear Auntie Em: Hate you! Hate Kansas!
Taking the dog. — Dorothy.

Eat one live toad the first thing in the
morning and nothing worse will happen to
you the rest of the day.

Eat well; stay fit; die anyway.

eBay is so useless. I tried to look up lighters
and all they had was 13,749 matches.

Education is important but other stuff is more
importanter.

If you believe that the quickest way to a
man's heart is the stomach, you know that
you are aiming a little too high.

I like kids, but I don't think I could eat a
whole one.

English is peculiar sometimes: incapable =
not capable. But inflammable = flammable.
And invaluable = very valuable.

Ever stop to think, and forget to start again?

Ever wonder about those people who spend $2.00 apiece on those little bottles of Evian water? Evian backwards is "Naive."

What's the difference between roast beef and pea soup? Anyone can roast beef.

Where do you find a dog with no legs? Right where you left him.

Teacher: "Where was the Constitution of India signed?" Student: "At the bottom of the page!"

It's cleaning day so naturally, I've already polished off a whole chocolate bar.

My dream job would be driving the karma bus.

If you can stay calm while all around you is chaos, then you probably haven't completely understood the situation.

When someone donates one kidney, he's hailed as a hero. I donated five and got arrested.

Do illiterate people get the full effect of alphabet soup?

Every day more money is printed for Monopoly than the US Treasury.

"Santa Claus has the right idea. Visit people only once a year." (Victor Borge)

I was in a job interview today. The manager handed me his laptop and said, "I want you to try to sell this to me." So, I put it under my arm, walked out of the building and went home. Eventually he called my cell phone and demanded, "Bring it back her, right now"! I said, "$200 and it's yours."

"Proof that we don't understand death is that we give dead people a pillow." (Jerry Seinfeld)

Every morning is the dawn of a new error.

My psychiatrist told me I was crazy, and I said I wanted a second opinion. He said, "Okay, you're ugly too!"

Every time I discover the meaning of life, they change it.

Every time you talk to your wife, you should remember that... 'This conversation will be recorded for Quality and Training purposes.'

Everybody is somebody else's weirdo.

A dog has an owner. A cat has a staff.

My doctor asked if anyone in my family suffers from mental illness. I said, "No, we all seem to enjoy it.

A dung beetle walks into a bar and asks, 'Is this stool taken?'

My parents are always telling me that their world doesn't revolve around me. I guess that means that I'm not actually their sun.

You must have been born on a highway because that's where most accidents happen.

When someone asks you, "A penny for your thoughts" and you put your two cents in ... what happens to the other penny?

A fine is a tax for doing wrong. A tax is a fine for doing well.

Ever wonder what the speed of lightning would be if it didn't zigzag?

Everyone has experienced that awkward moment when you leave a store without buying anything and all you can think is 'Act natural, you're innocent."

What do fish say when they hit a concrete wall? "Dam!"

With my luck, I'll probably be reincarnated as me.

Women marry because they believe that he will change one day. Men marry because they believe she'll never change. Both are mistaken.

Wouldn't it be ironic if Popeye's Chicken was fried in Olive Oil?

Everything happens for a reason; unfortunately, sometimes the reason is you.

Everywhere is walking distance if you have the time.

Exaggeration is a billion times worse than understatement.

I wear two pairs of pants when I go golfing. People ask me why and I tell them, "It's just in case I get a hole-in-one."

I went on a date with a blonde last night. "Do you have any kids?" she asked. "Yes," I replied. "I have one child that's just under two." She said, "I might be blonde, but I know how many one is."

I'm reading a horror story in Braille. Something bad is about to happen... I can feel it.

Experience is what you get when you didn't get what you wanted.

Facts do not cease to exist because they are ignored.

Failure is not an option. It's bundled with your software.

Fat Penguin. Excuse me. I just wanted to say something that breaks the ice.

What do you call a boomerang that doesn't work? A stick.

What do you call a dinosaur with an extensive vocabulary? A thesaurus

Few women admit their age; few men act it.

Fighting for peace is like screwing for virginity.

Finland has just closed it borders... so now nobody can cross the Finnish line.

First woman: "My son came to visit for summer vacation." Second woman: "How nice! Did you meet him at the airport?" First woman: "Oh, no. I've known him for years!"

Following the rules will not get the job done.

What do you call a bagel that can fly? A plain bagel.

For a while, Houdini used a trap door in every single one of his shows. I guess you could say it was a stage he was going through.

For every action, there is a corresponding over-reaction.

For Halloween we dressed up as almonds. Everyone could tell we were nuts.

Everybody repeat after me: "We are all individuals."

Everyone has a photographic memory. Some just don't have film.

When tempted to fight fire with fire, remember that the Fire Department usually uses water.

When wearing a bikini, women reveal 90 % of their body. Men are so polite they only look at the covered parts.

Everyone seems normal until you get to know them.

Forget about world peace. Visualize using your turn signal!

Four fonts walk into a bar. The bartender says, 'Hey! We don't want your type in here!'

Ghosts are bad liars because they're easy to see through.

Give a man a fish and he will eat for a day. Teach him how to fish, and he will sit in a boat and drink beer all day.

When a man opens the door of his car for his wife, you can be sure of one thing: either the car is new, or the wife is.

My brain has two parts – left and right. In the left side, there's nothing right. And in the right side, there's nothing left.

There are two rules for success: 1) Don't tell all you know.

There are two types of guys: those who pee in the shower and those who don't admit it.

There is a new trend in our office. Everyone is putting names on their food. I saw it today, while I was eating a sandwich named 'Kevin'.

Love is the triumph of imagination over intelligence.

What happens if you get scared half to death twice?

Give me ambiguity or give me something else.

Good health is merely the slowest possible rate at which one can die.

I've been repeating the same mistakes in life for so long now, I think I'll start calling them traditions.

I've got a phobia of over-engineered buildings. It's a complex complex complex.

What happens to an illegally parked frog? It gets toad.

Honesty is the best policy, but insanity is the best defense.

The future, the present, and the past walk into a bar. Things got a little tense.

The gene pool could use a little chlorine.

For chemists, alcohol is not a problem, it's a solution.

A diplomat is someone who can tell you to go to hell in such a way that you will look forward to the trip.

I'm reading a book about anti-gravity. I just can't put it down.

Whenever I try to eat healthy, a chocolate bar looks at me and Snickers.

Why was six afraid of seven? Because seven ate nine.

The grass may be greener on the other side, but at least I don't have to mow it.

Google is definitely a woman. It starts suggesting things before you can even finish your sentence.

I had too much wine last night. I have no idea how I got home from the sofa.

If you think you're old, you will be old. Think you are young, and you will be...delusional.

Give a man a gun and he will rob a bank. Give a man a bank and he will rob everyone.

Honestly, it's not the way I look that reveals my age. It's my use of complete sentences when I text.

Ham and Eggs: A day's work for a chicken, a lifetime commitment for a pig.

Having nutrition information on a bag of Cheetos is like having dating tips on a box of Crocs.

The consumption of alcohol is a major factor in dancing like a retarded person.

Whatever you do, always give 100% . . . unless you're donating blood.

Everything can be filed under "miscellaneous."

Why isn't the number 11 pronounced onety one?

I used to think I was indecisive. But now I'm not so sure.

A Woman's Rule of Thumb: If it has tires or testicles, you're going to have trouble with it.

He's slower than a herd of turtles stampeding through peanut butter.

He's as sharp as a bowling ball. After kissing his girlfriend on her sofa, she said, "Let's take this upstairs." "Ok," he said, you grab one end and I'll grab the other."

Hell hath no fury like a mother who sees her child using plates reserved for guests only.

Hello everyone, welcome to Plastic Surgery Addicts Anonymous. I see a lot of new faces here tonight.

Help stamp out, eliminate, and abolish redundancy!

Here's to alcohol - the solution for all of life's problems.

What do you call birds that stick together? Vel-crows.

What is sticky and brown? A stick.

Honey is the only food that doesn't spoil.

What is the difference between a Harley and a Hoover? The location of the dirt bag.

I named my hard drive 'dat ass' so once a month my computer asks if I want to 'back dat ass up'.

"One time my whole family played hide and seek. They found my mother in Pittsburgh!" (Rodney Dangerfield)

"Only Irish coffee provides in a single glass all four essential food groups: alcohol, caffeine, sugar and fat." (Alex Levine)

Nothing is impossible. The word itself says 'I'm possible.'

What do you call a boomerang that doesn't work? A stick.

What do you call a fake noodle? An impasta.

Hey, you have something on your chin... no, the 3rd one down.

Which one of these is the non-smoking lifeboat?

While acquainting myself with a new elderly patient, I asked, "How long have you been bedridden?" After a look of complete confusion she answered, "Why, not for about twenty years—when my husband was alive."

Hello, you've reached 1-800-NARCISSIST, how can you help me?

White smoke from under my hood means either my starter went out or my car has elected a new Pope.

Treat each day as if it's your last, and one day you'll be right.

Turning vegan would be a big missed steak.

Cleaning your house while your kids are still growing is like clearing the driveway before it's stopped snowing.

Two antennas met on a roof, fell in love, and got married. The ceremony wasn't much, but the reception was excellent.

Hippopotomonstrosesquippedaliophobia is the fear of long words.

His girlfriend, Ruth, fell off the back of his motorcycle. He just rode on - Ruthless.

Honk if you've never seen an Uzi fired from a car window.

Hospitality: making your guests feel like they're at home, even if you wish they were.

What do you call skydiving lawyers? Skeet.

Treat two-faced people like mushrooms. Keep them in the dark and feed them shit.

Only after getting married do you realize that those husband-wife jokes were not just jokes.

Only dead fish go with the flow.

"Money can't buy you happiness ... but it does bring you a more pleasant form of misery." (Spike Milligan)

Some people call me crazy. I prefer happy with a twist.

How are tornadoes and marriage alike? They both begin with a lot of sucking and blowing, and in the end, you lose your house.

Nothing says' I love my dog' quite like spending more money on his haircut than you do your own.

How do trees get online? They just log on.

How do you know if someone is hitchhiking or just complimenting your driving?

How is a government worker like a shotgun with a broken firing pin? It doesn't work, and you can't fire it.

When you replace W with T in 'where', 'when' and 'what', you get precisely the answers to those questions.

Whenever someone calls me ugly, I get super sad and hug them, because I know how tough life is for the visually impaired.

How is it that I always seem to buy the plants without the will to live?

Humans and dolphins are the only species that have sex for pleasure.

When the bosses talk about improving productivity, they are never talking about themselves.

"My luck is so bad that if I bought a cemetery, people would stop dying." (Rodney Dangerfield)

Husband: "Scientists have found that men say about 10,000 words a day, while women say about 20,000." Wife (shouting from the kitchen): "That's because we have to repeat everything twice for you blockheads." Husband: "What?"

I accidentally handed my wife a glue stick instead of a ChapStick. She still isn't talking to me.

I accidentally pooped my pants in the elevator. I'm taking this shit to a whole new level.

Whatever I did to piss you off, please let me know so I can do it again.

I always feel better when my doctor says something is normal for my age, but then I realize that, at some point, dying will also be normal for my age.

I always take life with a grain of salt. And a slice of lemon. And a shot of tequila.

Want to get noticed? Go jogging without moving your arms.

How to lose an argument with a woman: 1) Argue.

I always wanted to be a procrastinator. I just never got around to it.

"My wife has a slight impediment in her speech. Every now and then she stops to breathe." (Jimmy Durante)

I am a nutritional overachiever...but I am having an out of money experience.

I am in shape. Round is a shape.

I am not afraid of heights...just widths.

What do you call a priest who becomes a lawyer? A father-in-law.

What's a frog's favorite type of shoes? Open toad sandals.

Women spend more time wondering what men are thinking than men spend thinking.

I am not the kind of girl you can take home to your wife.

I am on a seafood diet. Every time I see food, I eat it.

I ask people why they have deer heads on their walls. They always say because it's such a beautiful animal. I think my mother is attractive, but I only have photographs of her.

The only knowledge that can hurt you is the knowledge you don't have.

The only substitute for good manners is fast reflexes.

The only thing wrong with a perfect drive to work is that you end up at work.

My wife still hasn't told me what my New Year's resolutions are.

Doing yoga got me out of the habit of biting my fingernails. Now I bite my toenails.

This is my step ladder. I never knew my real ladder.

My wife ran after the garbage truck, yelling, "Am I too late for the garbage?" The driver turned around and said, "No, jump in!"

When you stop believing in Santa Claus is when you start getting clothes for Christmas.

Women sometimes make fools of men, but most guys are the do-it-yourself type.

This isn't working out. I think we should start making other people miserable.

Ordinarily people live and learn. You just live.

Our child has a great deal of willpower—and even more won't power.

Those that forget the pasta are doomed to reheat it.

Which sexual position produces the ugliest children? Ask your mother.

Those who live by the sword get shot by those who don't.

One day I'll look up from my phone and realize my kids put me in a nursing home.

One day you're the best thing since sliced bread. The next, you're toast.

I asked my wife, "Where do you want to go for our anniversary?" She said, "Somewhere I have never been." I told her, "How about the kitchen?"

We always hold hands. If I let go, she shops.

Whenever you get mad, just think of a t-rex trying to masturbate.

When my wife told me to stop impersonating a flamingo, I had to put my foot down.

I can tell when people are being judgmental just by looking at them.

I can't get enough minimalism.

I can't believe I got fired from the calendar factory. All I did was take a day off.

I changed my iPod's name to Titanic. It's syncing now.

The sole purpose of a child's middle name is so he can tell when he's really in trouble.

The sooner you fall behind, the more time you'll have to catch up.

The state with the highest percentage of people who walk to work is Alaska.

I cooked Pancakes this morning. I was thrilled, but my kids weren't. Apparently, he was their favorite rabbit.

I could be a morning person... if morning started around noon.

I don't have an attitude. I have a personality you can't handle.

Sorry I'm late. I was trying to think of ways to get out of this.

When you're driving, have you ever noticed that anybody going slower than you is an idiot, and anyone going faster is a maniac?

My wife sent me a text that that said, "your great." So, naturally I wrote back, "No, you're great." She's been walking around all happy and smiling. Should I tell her that I was just correcting her grammar or leave it alone?

Statistically 6 out of 7 dwarfs are not Happy.

Stop repeat offenders. Don't re-elect them!

Stress is when you wake up screaming and you realize you haven't fallen asleep yet.

I don't trust English. Why is it that "give her her book is correct, yet give him him book is incorrect? Is English female?

Scientists say the universe is made up of protons, neurons, and electrons. They forgot to mention morons.

My wife was furious at me for kicking dropped ice cubes under the refrigerator. But now it's just water under the fridge.

I entered what I ate today into my new fitness app, and it sent an ambulance to my house.

I finally got 8 hours of sleep. It took me three days, but …whatever.

I finally got my head together. Now my body is falling apart.

I find it ironic that the colors red, white, and blue stand for freedom until they are flashing behind you.

When wearing bikinis, women reveal 90% of their bodies. Men are so polite— they only look at the covered parts.

My wife was in beauty salon for two hours That was only for the estimate. She got a mudpack and looked great for two days. Then the mud fell off.

Men can read smaller print than women can; women can hear better.

I found a rock yesterday which measured 1760 yards in length. Must be some kind of milestone.

What's the difference between a jeweler and a jailer? One sells watches and the other watches cells.

Which sexual position produces the ugliest children? Ask your mother.

I got lost in your eyes. But I also get lost in most department stores, so I wouldn't read too much into it.

I grew up with Bob Hope, Steve Jobs and Johnny Cash. Now there are no Jobs, no Cash and no Hope.

I had a date last night. It was perfect. Tomorrow I'll try a grape.

I had prepared for a battle of wits, but I see you came unarmed.

I hate cocaine dealers. They're always sticking their business into other people's noses.

I hate it when people don't know the difference between 'your' and 'you're.' Their so stupid.

I hate sex in the movies. Only tried it once, and the seat folded up.

I hate this snow! No... wait... I love this snow! Signed, Bi-Polar Bear

I have kleptomania. When it gets bad, I take something for it.

I have many jokes about unemployed people. Sadly, none of them work.

There are few things I enjoy more than picking an argument with my girlfriend when she has the hiccups.

There are two kinds of friends: those who are always around when you need them, and those who are only around when they need you.

There is no key to a woman's heart. There's only a password that changes regularly.

I have not met a single person who was happily married.

Every time someone calls me fat, I get so depressed I cut myself... a piece of cake.

The adult version of "head shoulders, knees and toes" is "wallet, glasses, keys and phone."

I have only seen people underwhelmed or overwhelmed, never whelmed properly.

I have six locks on my door all in a row. When I go out, I lock every other one. I figure no matter how long somebody stands there picking the locks, they are always locking three.

The ant can lift 50 times its own weight, can pull 30 times its own weight and always fails over on its right side when intoxicated.

I heard there were a bunch of break-ins over at the car park. That is wrong on so many levels.

I hope when I inevitably choke to death on gummy bears people just say I was killed by bears and leave it at that.

I invented a new word today: Plagiarism.

I just read that alligators can grow up to 15 feet. But I haven't seen any with more than 4.

I know a guy who is really poor. When I saw him kicking a can across the street, I asked him what he was doing. He said, "Moving."

I know a guy who's addicted to brake fluid, but he says he can stop any time.

My wife had her driver's test the other day. She got 8 out of 10. The other 2 guys jumped clear.

I know Jiu-Jitsu, Sambo, Judo, Aikido... and lots of other scary words.

I lost my job at the bank on my very first day. A woman asked me to check her balance, so I pushed her over.

I love cats...they taste just like chicken.

My wife is threatening to leave me because of my obsession with wearing different clothes every few hours. I said, "Wait, I can change."

What did E.T.'s mother say to him when he got home? "Where on Earth have you been?"

There are 3 guys on a boat with 4 cigarettes, but they have nothing to light them with, so they throw a cigarette overboard and the boat becomes a cigarette lighter.

There are approximately 45 seconds between "I'll make us an omelet" and "We're having scrambled eggs."

I love what you've done with your hair. How do you get it to come out of your nostrils like that?

My wife had me take out more life insurance and now there's no grip left on the bathmat. Weird.

I may not be in a relationship, but I am three people's plan B and one person's 'maybe if we're ever the last two people on Earth.'

Don't bother walking a mile in my shoes; that would be boring. Instead, spend 30 seconds in my head. That'll freak you right out!

I asked my wife what she's "burning up for dinner" and it turned out to be all of my personal belongings.

Friends may come and go, but enemies accumulate.

Geology rocks, but geography's where it's at.

Don't spell part backwards. It's a trap.

What do you call two birds in love?
Tweethearts.

Don't you hate it when someone answers
their own questions? I do.

Double negatives are a No-No in English.

I found out I'm colorblind. The diagnosis
came completely out of the purple.

My girlfriend is always stealing my t-shirts
and sweaters... But if I take one of her
dresses, suddenly 'we need to talk.'

I may not be the brightest nail in the bucket,
but at least I have a point.

I met my soulmate. She didn't.

My annoying little cousin keeps bragging
about how he sleeps in a racecar bed. Well,
the joke's on you, little fella, I sleep in a real
car.

My bed wasn't feeling well this morning, so I
had to stay home to take care of it.

What hair color do they put on the driver's
licenses of bald men?

Always remember that you are unique...just like everyone else.

I named my dog 'Five Miles' so I could tell people that I walk 5 miles every day.

I need to start paying closer attention to stuff. Today I found out that my wife and I have separate names for the cat.

I never knew what happiness was until I got married—and then it was too late.

Why do we sing *'Take me out to the ball game'* when we're already there?

Why are they called "stands" when they're made for sitting?

Why is it called "after dark" when it's really "after light?"

Doesn't "expecting the unexpected" make the unexpected expected?

My girlfriend isn't talking to me. She said I ruined her birthday. I'm not sure how. I didn't even know it was her birthday.

Why is "phonics" not spelled the way it sounds?

The difference between "Girlfriend" and "Girl Friend" is that little space in between we call the "Friend Zone".

If work is so terrific, why do they have to pay you to do it?

If all the world is a stage, where is the audience sitting?

I never make mistakes. I thought I did once, but I was wrong.

I often confuse reptiles and amphibians. Actually, to be honest, they pretty much never know what I'm talking about.

I ordered a chicken and an egg from Amazon. I'll let you know.

I put my grandma on speed dial the other day. I call it Insta-gram.

I read recipes the same way I read science fiction. I get to the end, and I think, 'Well, that's not going to happen.'

I read that 4,153,237 people got married last year. Not to cast doubt on that figure, but shouldn't that be an even number?

Why are a 'wise man' and a 'wise guy' opposites?

Why do 'overlook' and 'oversee' mean opposite things?

My doctor told me that jogging could add years to my life. He was right—I feel ten years older already.

My dog and I both freak out whenever the doorbell rings, but we run in opposite directions.

I received a call from the school telling me my son is constantly lying. I said, "Tell him he's a good liar. I don't have a son."

I recently decided to sell my vacuum cleaner — all it was doing was gathering dust.

I run like the winded.

No one is listening until you fart.

I saw a guy on his motorcycle and the back of his shirt said, 'If you can read this the bitch fell off.'

My luck is like a bald guy who just won a comb.

I saw my dad chopping up onions today and I cried. Onions was a good dog.

I sometimes go to my own little world, but that's okay; they know me there.

I sometimes watch birds and wonder, 'If I could fly who would I shit on?'

i souport publik edukashun.

I spent a lot of time, money, and effort child-proofing my house ... but the kids still get in.

I started out with nothing and I still have most of it.

I take my wife everywhere, but she keeps finding her way back.

Don't squat with spurs on.

I think my coworkers are gay. Every time I walk by, they mumble, "What an ass!"

I think my dog always follows me to the bathroom because I always follow him outside, and he thinks that's the way it works.

Why are there 5 syllables in the word 'monosyllabic'?

Why are they called 'hemorrhoids? They should be called 'asteroids'.

I think my girlfriend has a blind fetish. Last night she said we should stop seeing each other.

I told my niece that I saw a moose on the way to work this morning. She said, "How do you know he was on his way to work?"

Age 60 might be the new 40, but 9 PM is the new midnight.

I told my suitcases there will be no holiday this year. Now I'm dealing with the emotional baggage.

Why do a Pilgrim's pants always fall down? Because they wear their belt buckles on their hats.

Why do gorillas have big nostrils? Because they have big fingers.

I told my wife I wanted to be cremated. She made me an appointment for Tuesday.

I'm on two diets. I wasn't getting enough food on one.

On average, right-handed people live nine years longer than left-handed people do.

I told my wife she should embrace her mistakes...so she hugged me.

I used to be in a band. We were called 'Lost Dog'. You probably saw our posters.

I used to have a handle on life, but then it broke.

Why is the man who invests all your money called a broker?

I walked past a homeless guy with a sign that read, 'One day, this could be you.' I put my money back in my pocket just in case he's right.

I want to die peacefully in my sleep, like my grandfather... Not screaming and yelling like the passengers in his car.

I want to grow my own food...but I can't find bacon seeds.

What did one DNA say to the other DNA?
"Do these genes make me look fat?"

What did the buffalo say when his son left for college? Bison.

I wanted to lose 10 pounds this year. Only 13 to go.

I was a diesel fitter at a pantyhose factory. As they came off the line, I would hold them up and say, "Yeah, Deez'l fit her."

I was going to quit all my bad habits for the new year, but then I remembered that nobody likes a quitter.

When you ask me what I'm doing today, and I say 'nothing', it doesn't mean that I'm free. It means I'm doing nothing.

People tend to make rules for others and exceptions for themselves.

When you do squats, are your knees supposed to sound like a goat chewing on an aluminum can stuffed with celery?

When you don't know what you're doing, it's best, to do it quickly.

When you don't know what to do, walk fast and look worried.

I was riding a donkey the other day when someone threw a rock at me, and I fell off. I guess I was stoned off my ass.

I was thinking about how people seem to read the Bible a whole lot more as they get older; then it dawned on me ... they're cramming for their final exam.

I was wondering why the frisbee kept getting bigger and bigger, but then it hit me.

I wasn't originally going to get a brain transplant, but then I changed my mind.

My psychology professor asked if we had heard of Pavlov. I said, "It rings a bell." No one laughed. I'm way too witty for this class.

I waved to a man because I thought he had waved at me. Apparently, he'd waved to another woman. So, to get out of the awkward situation, I kept my hand up and a taxi pulled over and drove me to the airport. I'm now in Poland starting a new life.

I went swimming today. I took a pee in the deep end. The lifeguard noticed and blew his f**king whistle so loud, I almost fell in.

I went to a seafood disco last week but ended up pulling a mussel.

What is the difference between a unicorn and a carrot? One is a funny beast and the other is a bunny feast.

What is the difference between snowmen and snowwomen? Snowballs.

What word becomes 'shorter' when you add two letters to it? Short.

I work in a library. Literally, all we do is judge books by their covers.

I work out almost every day. Friday I almost worked out, Saturday I almost worked out, Sunday I almost worked out....

I would love to live in a world where people came with on/off switches.

I, for one, like Roman numerals.

I WRITE ALL MY JOKES IN CAPITALS. THIS ONE WAS WRITTEN IN PARIS.

The three unwritten rules of life: 1. 2. 3.

The trouble with being punctual is that nobody's there to appreciate it.

The trouble with doing something right the first time is that nobody appreciates how difficult it was.

A friend of mine tried to annoy me with bird puns, but I soon realized that toucan play that game.

I went to school to become a wit, but I only got halfway through.

I'd like to see things from your point of view, but I can't seem to get my head that far up my ass.

I'm attracted to women who are beautiful when they're angry, because once we start dating, that's how they'll look 90% of the time.

I'm busy now. Can I ignore you some other time?

I'm currently boycotting any company that sells items I can't afford.

I'm great at multitasking. I can waste time, be unproductive, and procrastinate all at once.

I'm here for whatever you need me to do from the couch.

I'm jealous of all the people that haven't met you.

A garage sale is actually a garbage sale, but the 'b' is silent.

I'm multi-talented: I can talk and piss you off at the same time.

I'm not into working out. My philosophy: No pain, no pain.

A ghost walked into a bar and ordered a shot of vodka. The bartender said, 'Sorry, we don't serve spirits here.'

I'm not saying I hate you, but I would unplug your life support to charge my phone.

A good wife always forgives her husband when she's wrong.

I'm not saying your perfume is too strong. I'm just saying the canary was alive before you got here.

"Maybe it's true that life begins at fifty, but everything else starts to wear out, fall out, or spread out." (Phyllis Diller)

Remember when "It's complicated" was a relationship status, not a gender?

I'm terrified of elevators and I'm taking steps to avoid them.

The first time I got a universal remote control, I thought to myself, 'This changes everything!'

The four most essential words for a healthy, vital relationship: "I apologize." And "You're right."

Remember, it's not what you do... it's what you get away with.

I've always had an irrational fear of speed bumps, but I'm slowly getting over it.

I'm so poor I can't even pay attention.

You can go anywhere you want if you look serious and carry a clipboard.

You can judge the character of a man by how he treats those who can do nothing for him.

What does a liar do after he dies? He lies still.

What does the man in the moon do when his hair got too long? Eclipse it.

What goes 'clop, clop, clop, bang, bang, clop, clop clop? An Amish drive-by shooting.

"The worst time to have a heart attack is during a game of charades." (Demetri Martin)

"Until I was thirteen, I thought my name was "SHUT UP." (Joe Namath)

I've only been wrong once, and that's when I thought I was wrong.

Remember, children... the best way to get a puppy for Christmas is to beg for a baby brother.

If a cow laughed, would milk come out of her nose?

I'm writing a book about all the things I should be doing with my life. It's an oughtobiography.

I've reached the age where my train of thought often leaves the station without me.

If 4 out of 5 people *suffer* from diarrhea... does that mean that one enjoys it?

If a man speaks in the forest and there is no woman there to hear it... is he still wrong?

If a statue in the park of a person on a horse has both front legs in the air, the person died in battle. If the horse has one front leg in the air, the person died as the result of wounds received in battle. If the horse has all four legs on the ground, the person died of natural causes.

When people won't talk to me, it doesn't bother me. When a dog won't let me pet them, that really hurts.

If at first you don't succeed, destroy all evidence that you tried.

I've pre-planned my funeral to include a 32-minute montage of the times I've accidentally waved hello to someone waving to someone behind me.

When someone asks me if I'm seeing anyone, I automatically assume they're talking about a psychiatrist.

You are slower than a herd of turtles stampeding through peanut butter.

Why don't blind people like to skydive? Because it scares the hell out of the dog

The word 'umbrella' was going to be just 'brella' but the inventor of the word hesitated.

If all is lost, where is it?

You are so old. When you were a kid rainbows were black and white.

If at first you don't succeed, skydiving is probably not for you.

If attacked by a mob of clowns, go for the juggler.

You bring everyone a lot of joy...when you leave the room.

You can never lose a homing pigeon. If your homing pigeon doesn't come back, what you've lost is a pigeon.

If every day is a gift, I'd like a receipt for Monday. I want to exchange it for another Friday.

What did one traffic light say to the other? Stop looking! I'm changing!

You are more likely to be killed by a champagne cork than by a poisonous spider.

You are proof that evolution can go in reverse.

If God wanted me to touch my toes, He would've put them on my knees.

No matter how much you push the envelope, it'll still be stationery.

If some people didn't tell you, you'd never know they'd been away on vacation.

If the Jacksonville Jaguars are known as the "Jags" and the Tampa Bay Buccaneers are known as the "Bucs," what does that make the Tennessee Titans?

Never laugh at your girlfriend's choices... you're one of them.

Never underestimate a woman's ability to make anything your fault.

Never tell your problems to anyone...20% don't care and the other 80% are glad you have them. Come on

No matter how bad you're playing, it's always possible to play worse.

Not all men are annoying. Some are dead.

If the right side of the brain controls the left side of the body, then lefties are the only ones in their right mind.

If there was a pill to cure procrastination, I'd probably take it tomorrow.

No NFL team which plays its home games in a domed stadium has ever won a Super Bowl.

No one ever says, "It's only a game" when their team is winning.

No one is listening until you make a mistake.

If there was a pill to cure procrastination, I'd probably take it tomorrow.

What's the difference between men and government bonds? Bonds mature.

If we aren't supposed to eat animals, why are they made of meat?

What's the difference between the Pope and your boss? The Pope only expects you to kiss his ring.

If you drink, don't park; accidents cause people.

What's the difference between ignorance and apathy? I don't know, and I don't care.

If you eat yeast and shoe polish every morning you will rise and shine.

Do I lose when the police officer says papers and I say scissors?

Do infants enjoy infancy as much as adults enjoy adultery?

Do Lipton Tea employees take coffee breaks?

Why do you press harder on the buttons of a remote control when you know the batteries are dead?

Why do we put suits in garment bags and garments in a suitcase?

If you fart consistently for 6 years and 9 months, enough gas is produced to create the energy of an atomic bomb.

If you lend someone $20, and never see that person again, it was probably worth it.

If you lived in your car, you'd be home by now.

If you lose a sock in the dryer, it comes back as a Tupperware lid that doesn't fit any of your containers.

If you put your left shoe on the wrong foot... it's on the right foot.

If you see me talking to myself, just move along. I'm self-employed and we're having a staff meeting.

If you take an Oriental person and spin him around several times, does he become disoriented?

If you tell the truth, you don't have to remember anything.

If you think nobody cares whether you're alive, try missing a couple of mortgage payments.

I always wondered what the job application form is like at Hooters. Do they just give you a bra and say, "Here, fill this out?"

What's the fastest way to a man's heart? Through his chest with a sharp knife.

I can't understand why women are okay with the fact that JC Penney has an older women's clothing line named 'Sag Harbor.'

The location of your mailbox shows you how far away from your house you can go in a robe before you start looking like a mental patient.

If you're going to be two faced, at least make one of them pretty.

At every party there are two kinds of people: those who want to go home and those who don't. The trouble is, they are usually married to each other.

If you're struggling to remember a word, just say, "I can't remember the English word for it." That wav people will think you're bilingual, instead of an idiot.

If you're happy and you know it, it's your meds.

If you're sitting in public and a stranger sits down next to you, just stare straight ahead and say, "Did you bring the money?"

If your dog is barking at the back door and your wife is yelling at the front door, who do you let in first? The dog of course. At least he'll shut up after you let him in.

Important letters that contain no errors will develop errors in the email.

Impotence is nature's way of saying "No hard feelings."

Sometimes, when I close my eyes, I can't see.

I once met an honest, caring, politician that listened when I spoke and tried to help the country. Then I woke up.

I ordered 2000 lbs. of Chinese soup. It was Won Ton.

Sometimes, when I'm cruising the city in a $200K vehicle, I lean back and think, "If the bus driver doesn't speed up, I'll be late for work."

Improve your memory by doing unforgettable things.

In 40 years, we'll have thousands of old ladies running around with tattoos?

In ancient Egypt, Priests plucked every hair from their bodies, including their eyebrows and eyelashes.

If you're good, you'll be assigned all the work. If you're really good, you'll get out of it.

In English pubs, ale is ordered by pints and quarts. So, in old England, when customers got unruly, the bartender would yell at them to mind their own pints and quarts and settle down. It's where we get the phrase "mind your P's and Q's".

In English, to leave a party without telling anyone is called a "French Exit". In French, it's called a "partir a l'anglaise", to leave like the English.

In just two days, tomorrow will be yesterday.

Afraid of Santa? You may be Claustrophobic.

In order to be a smartass, you must first be smart. Otherwise, you're just an ass.

In Shakespeare's time, mattresses were secured on bed frames by ropes. When you pulled on the ropes the mattress tightened, making the bed firmer to sleep on. Hence the phrase, "Good night, sleep tight."

Indecision is the key to flexibility.

In the beginning, God created earth… and rested. Then God created man… and rested. Then God created woman… and since then, neither God nor man has rested.

Incorrectly is the only word that when spelled right, is still spelled incorrectly.

Instead of getting married again, I'm going to find a woman I don't like and give her a house.

Intelligence is like underwear. It's important that you have it, but not necessary that you show it off.

Is everything expensive or am I just poor?

If we shouldn't eat at night, why do they put a light in the fridge?

Is it good if a vacuum really sucks?

Why is the third hand on the watch called the second hand?

Intelligent people have more zinc and copper in their hair.

Is your ass jealous of the amount of shit that just came out of your mouth?

Isn't it weird how when a cop drives by you feel paranoid instead of protected?

It feels like we're living in the "Days Leading Up To..." section of the history books.

It hurts to be on the cutting edge.

Did you hear about the absent-minded policeman? He jumped off his whistle and blew his horse.

Did you hear about the guy whose whole left side got amputated? He's all right now.

It is better to understand a little than to misunderstand a lot.

It is easier to get older than it is to get wiser.

It is far more impressive when others discover your good qualities without your help.

It is much easier to apologize than to ask permission.

It matters not whether you win or lose. What matters is whether *I* win or lose.

It takes a lot of balls to golf the way I do.

It was the accepted practice in Babylon 4,000 years ago that for a month after the wedding, the bride's father would supply his son-in-law with all the mead he could drink. Mead is a honey beer. Because their calendar was lunar based, this period was called the honey month or what we now call the 'honeymoon.'

It's a good thing farts aren't contagious like yawns.

It's a small world… so you've got to use your elbows a lot.

It's not the fall that kills you; it's the sudden stop at the end.

It's so simple to be wise. Just think of something stupid to say and then don't say it.

It's the start of a brand-new day, and I'm off like a herd of turtles.

Just a warning: If you're buying a watch on Amazon, don't learn the hard way like I did. If it says you can swim with it, it only means if you can swim without it.

Why do we say something is out of whack? What is a whack?

Why do "slow down" and "slow up" mean the same thing?

It may be that your sole purpose in life is simply to serve as a warning to others.

Just accept it: Some days you're the pigeon and some days you're the statue.

How can you spot the blind guy at the nudist colony? It's not hard.

How do I disable the autocorrect function on my wife?

My wife and I are inseparable. In fact, last week it took four state troopers and a dog.

People say money is not the key to happiness, but I always figured if you had enough money, you could have a key made.

I don't want you to feel like you can't express yourself, but I do want you to stop talking.

How do people lose their kids at the mall? Seriously, any tips would be greatly appreciated.

I don't worry about terrorism. I was married for two years.

I don't mean to interrupt people. I just randomly remember things and I get really excited.

Why do "fat chance" and "slim chance" mean the same thing?

I don't suffer from stress. I'm a carrier.

I doubt, therefore I might be.

How can I miss you if you won't go away?

Just because I don't care doesn't mean I don't understand.

I just burned 2,000 calories. That's the last time I leave brownies in the oven while I nap.

I got fired from my job as a set designer. I left without making a scene.

Just tell me when and where and I'll be there 20 minutes late.

Justice is a dish best served cold because if it were served warm, it would be justwater.

Keep the dream alive: Hit the snooze button.

Knowledge is power, and power corrupts. So study hard and be evil.

Last night I lay in bed looking up at the stars in the sky, and I thought to myself, where the heck is the ceiling?

I don't have a solution, but I do admire the problem.

I have a chicken-proof lawn. It's impeccable.

Keep your eyes wide open before marriage, half shut afterwards.

Why do tugboats *push* their barges?

How do you make holy water? You boil the hell out of it.

Last night my girlfriend was complaining that I never listen to her... or something like that.

How do you throw a space party? You planet.

I have a dog to provide me with unconditional love, but I also have a cat to remind me that I don't deserve it. It's all about balance.

Laugh alone and the world thinks you're an idiot.

Lazy People Fact #5812672793. You were too lazy to read that number.

Life and beer are very similar. Chill for best results.

I got kicked out of a secret cooking society. I spilled the beans.

I read an article about the dangers of drinking that scared the crap out of me. That's it. No more reading!

Life isn't about winning and losing. It's about wishing you would have won and wondering why you lost.

Love is one long sweet dream... and marriage is the alarm clock.

Make it idiot proof and someone will make a better idiot.

Making a smoking section in a restaurant like making a peeing section in a swimming pool.

The introduction: He: "This is my ex-girlfriend, Lauren." She: "Stop introducing me like that. I'm his wife."

Many years ago in England, pub frequenters had a whistle baked into the rim or handle of their ceramic cups. When they needed a refill, they used the whistle to get some service. "Wet your whistle" is the phrase inspired by this practice.

Light travels faster than sound, which is the reason that some people appear bright before you hear them speak.

Marriage is like coffee. First, it's really hot. Then it's just right. Then it helps you to get off your ass and do things.

I let my mind wander, and it didn't come back.

Living on Earth is expensive, but it does include a free trip around the sun.

I just hired a private investigator to find out what I do all day.

Why is Christmas just like a day at the office? You do all the work and the fat guy with the suit gets all the credit.

Why is it everything I love is either unhealthy, addictive or have multiple restraining orders against me?

Psychoanalysis a lot quicker for men than for women because when it's time to go back to his childhood, he's already there.

I'm trying to date a philosophy professor, but she doesn't even know if I exist or not.

Marriage is a relationship in which one is always right and the other is the husband.

I'm trying to imagine you with a personality.

Losing a wife can be very tough. Some may even say impossible.

Everyone who is for abortion has already been born.

Materialism is buying things we don't need with money we don't have to impress people that don't matter.

Math Teacher: "If I have 5 bottles in one hand and 6 in the other hand, what do I have?"
Student: "A drinking problem."

Maybe if we start telling people their brain is an app, they'll want to use it.

Me: "Teacher, can I go to the bathroom?" Teacher: "It's may." Me: "No, It's February."

Men are always trying to convince women that 'guys' is a gender-neutral term, but when you ask them how many guys they've slept with, they take offense.

Men are fun to argue with, because even if they win, they lose.

I don't suffer from insanity—I enjoy every minute of it.

Money can't buy happiness, but it keeps the kids in touch.

Have you ever tried eating a clock? It's really time-consuming... especially if you go for seconds.

Love is blind but marriage is a real eye-opener.

Money talks ... but all mine ever says is 'good-bye.'

Moses was leading his people through the desert for 40 years. It seems, even in Biblical times, men avoided asking for directions.

Most people are shocked when they find out how bad I am as an electrician.

My girlfriend dressed up as a policewoman and told me I was under arrest on suspicion of being good in bed. After 2 minutes, all charges were dropped due to a lack of evidence.

My best friends and I played a game of hide and seek. It went on for hours because good friends are hard to find.

"As one person, I cannot change the world, but I can change the world of one person." (Paul Shane Spear)

What's the most dangerous part of a motorcycle? The nut that connects the seat to the handlebar.

"I met the surgeon general – he offered me a cigarette." (Rodney Dangerfield)

How many of you believe in telekinesis? Raise my hand!

My blond girlfriend said she was worried that her mechanic might try to rip her off, but she was relieved when he told her that all she needed was blinker fluid.

What's the difference between ignorance and apathy? I don't know and I don't care.

My boss is going to fire the employee with the worst posture. I have a hunch it might be me.

My boss said I intimidated the other employees, so I just stared at him until he apologized.

My buddy set me up on a blind date and said, "Just a heads up… she's expecting a baby." I felt like such an idiot sitting in the bar wearing just a diaper.

My calling in life went straight to voicemail.

I came, I saw, I forgot what I was doing. I retraced my steps and got lost on the way back. Now I have no idea what's going on.

I can cut down a tree only using my vision. It's true! I saw it with my own eyes!

I can only please one person per day. Today is not your day. Tomorrow is not looking good either.

My cross-eyed wife and I just got a divorce. We didn't see eye to eye. I also found out she was seeing someone on the side.

My dad told me his password is 'MickeyMinnieGoofyDonaldPlutoHueyLouie DeweyDublin because he was told his password had to contain 8 characters and at least one capital.

Why do I keep paying the bills? It just encourages them to send more.

Why do men die before their wives? They want to.

I want to make a joke about sodium, but Na.

Why do men name their penises? Because they don't like the idea of having a stranger make 90% of their decisions.

My dream woman has a special combination of inner and outer beauty and, most importantly, is too naive to know she's way out of my league.

I want to hang a map of the world in my house. Then I'm going to put pins into all the locations that I've traveled to. But first, I'm going to have to travel to the top two corners of the map, so it won't fall down.

When The Hulk goes off into a vicious rage and destroys everything, he's 'Incredible.' But when I do it, I'm 'an alcoholic.'

When the smog lifts in California, UCLA.

My friend got a job as senior director at Old McDonald's Farm. He's the CIEIO.

A cockroach can live nine days without its head, before it starves to death.

My grandfather tried to warn them about the Titanic. He screamed and shouted about the iceberg and how the ship was going to sink, but all they did was throw him out of the theater.

My IQ test results came back. They were negative.

My kids asked if they could do something and I said yes, so my wife lowered my security clearance and now I'm not authorized to make those decisions.

My kids have been throwing Scrabble tiles at each other again. It's all fun and games until someone loses an i.

I really don't mind getting old, but my body is having a major fit.

My love is like communism; everyone gets a share, and it's only good in theory.

I tried to explain to my 4-year-old son that it's perfectly normal to accidentally poop your pants...but he's still making fun of me.

A catfish has over 27,000 taste buds—the most of any animal.

I'm the type of person who tries to fall back asleep in the morning just to finish a dream.

I got a new pair of gloves, but they're both 'lefts' which, on the one hand, is great, but on the other, it's just not right.

My next house will have no kitchen — just vending machines.

A depression is a period during which we have to get along without the things our grandparents never dreamed of.

A diplomat is a man who always remembers a woman's birthday but never remembers her age.

My opinions may have changed, but not the fact that I'm right.

I assert dominance over millennials by responding to their texts with phone calls.

I ate a frozen apple. Hard core.

I bought you a calendar. Your days are numbered now.

My relationship with whiskey is on the rocks.

My speech today will be like a mini skirt. Long enough to cover the essentials but short enough to hold your attention.

I love deadlines. I especially like the whooshing sound they make as they go flying by.

I love the way the Earth rotates. It literally makes my day.

A man on a date wonders if he'll get lucky. A woman already knows.

My wife asked me earlier, "Are you even listening to me?"—which is a really weird way to start a conversation.

I picked up a hitchhiker. He asked if I wasn't afraid he might be a serial killer? I told him the odds of two serial killers being in the same car were extremely unlikely.

I went line dancing last night. OK, it was a roadside sobriety test. Same thing.

My wife dresses to kill. She cooks the same way.

The easiest time to add insult to injury is when you're signing someone's cast.

The evening news is where they begin with, 'Good evening'... and then proceed to tell you why it isn't.

I got in a fight one time with a really big guy, and he said, "I'm going to mop the floor with your face." I said, "You'll be sorry." He said, "Oh, yeah? Why?" I said, "Well, you won't be able to get into the corners very well."

I got lost in thoughts. It was unfamiliar territory.

My wife left me because I'm insecure. No, wait, she's back. She just went to get coffee.

I'd tell you a chemistry joke, but I know I wouldn't get a reaction.

My wife asked me to take her to one of those restaurants where they make food right in front of you. I took her to Subway.

I'm a humble person, really. I'm actually much greater than I think I am.

Never trust a man that says, "Trust me." and never trust a woman that says, "It's fine."

I had a job selling security alarms door to door and I was really good at it. If no one was home, I would just leave a brochure on the kitchen table.

I had my patience tested. I'm negative.

My wife set a limit on how much we can spend on each other for Christmas. It's $100 on me and $500 on her.

Necrophilia is that uncontrollable urge to crack open a cold one.

A flea can jump 350 times its body length. It's the equivalent of a human jumping the length of a football field.

Needing someone is like needing a parachute. If he isn't there the first time, chances are you won't be needing him again.

My friend was explaining electricity to me, but I was like, 'Watt?'

No one is listening until you fart.

Never argue with a woman when she's tired...or when she's rested.

My wife says she is no longer buying junk food for the family because, "Everyone just eats it."

Never ask a woman who is eating ice cream straight from the carton how she's doing.

No matter how much you push the envelope, it'll still be stationery.

If you want your spouse to listen and pay undivided attention to every word you say, talk in your sleep.

No matter how bad you're playing, it's always possible to play worse.

Never tell your problems to anyone. 20% don't care and the other 80% are glad you have them.

My friend's bakery burned down last night. Now his business is toast.

No NFL team which plays its home games in a domed stadium has ever won a Super Bowl.

No one has ever complained of a parachute not opening. Think about it.

My friends laughed at me when I told them I had a hot date. They said she was imaginary. Well, the jokes on them. They're imaginary, too!

Never give up...because that is just the time and place that the tide will turn.

Not all men are annoying. Some are dead.

If love is blind, why is lingerie so popular?

My girlfriend's such a bad cook, she uses the smoke alarm as a timer.

If you are cross-eyed and have dyslexia, can you read all right?

Not to brag, but my antics at work resulted in several items being added to the employee manual.

Nothing spoils the target more than a hit.

No woman ever falls in love with a man unless she has a better opinion of him than he deserves.

Why doesn't glue stick to the inside of the bottle?

No word in the English language rhymes with month, orange, silver or purple.

Nostalgia isn't what it used to be.

Why do they call it a TV 'set' when you only have one?

My silence doesn't mean I agree with you. It means your level of stupidity rendered me speechless.

Novak Djokovic is the first player to be knocked out of a Grand Slam tournament after missing only two shots.

Now that I'm older, I realize that my imaginary friend was really nothing more than an imaginary acquaintance.

Marriage is a three-ring circus—engagement ring - wedding ring, suffering.

Nurse: "Doctor, there's a patient on line one that says he's invisible." Doctor: "Well, tell him I can't see him right now."

Oh... I didn't tell you? Then it must be none of your business...

Old age comes at a bad time.

Good judgment comes from bad experience, and a lot of that comes from bad judgment.

Only two people signed the Declaration of Independence on July 4th—John Hancock and Charles Thomson. Most of the rest signed on August 2, but the last signature wasn't added until 5 years later.

Oxymorons: Found Missing; Open Secret; Small Crowd; Act Naturally; Fully Empty; Pretty Ugly; Original Copy; Only Choice; Liquid Gas; Social Distancing.

If by free spirits you mean an open bar, then yes, I love free spirits.

I asked the bus driver "How long will the next bus be?" He replied, "Same length as this one."

My sister bet me I couldn't make a car out of spaghetti. U should of seen her face as I drove pasta.

If elevators hadn't been invented, all the CEOs would have their offices on the first floor as a sign of status... and the entry level employees would be up on the 60th floor.

Patience is a virtue. It's just not one of *my* virtues.

Whatever you do, always give 100% . . . unless you're donating blood.

What do you call a sleepwalking nun? A Roamin' Catholic

I went to see the doctor about my short-term memory problems. The first thing he did was make me pay in advance.

I wonder how much deeper the ocean would be without sponges.

What did Snow White say when she came out of the photo booth? "Someday my prints will come."

A girl said she recognized me from her vegetarian club, but I'd never met herbivore.

Dad, are we pyromaniacs? Yes, we arson.

Why do you suppose kamikaze pilots wore helmets?

I think my neighbor is stalking me as she's been googling my name on her computer. I saw it through my telescope last night.

My son asked me what it's like to be married so I told him to leave me alone, and when he did, I asked him why he was ignoring me.

I threw out my back sleeping and tweaked my neck sneezing, so I'm probably just one strong fart away from complete paralysis.

I told him to be himself; that was pretty mean, I guess

People don't have a strong intuitive sense of how much bigger 1 billion is than 1 million. 1 million seconds is about 11.5 days. 1 billion seconds is about 31.75 years.

People who use selfie sticks really need to have a good, long look at themselves.

I know they say that money talks, but all mine says is 'Goodbye.'

I like birthdays but too many can kill you.

People who want to share their religious or political views with you almost never want you to share yours with them.

Photons have mass? I didn't even know they were Catholic.

Politics is the art of looking for trouble, finding it, misdiagnosing it, and then misapplying the wrong remedies.

I like kids, but I don't think I could eat a whole one.

Pollen is what happens when flowers can't keep it in their plants.

Practice safe eating. Always use condiments.

Punctuation is important! A woman, without her man, is nothing. A woman: without her, man is nothing.

How do you weigh an elephant? It's just like weighing a person, but on a much larger scale.

I like older men because they've gotten used to life's disappointments... which means they're ready for me.

Marriage is the main reason for divorce.

Puns about communism aren't funny unless everyone gets them.

The most popular boat name is 'Obsession.'

What has a whole bunch of little balls and screws old ladies? Bingo machines.

Can a woman make you a millionaire? Yes... if you're a billionaire.

How do crazy people go through the forest? They take the psychopath.

"By the time a man is wise enough to watch his step, he's too old to go anywhere." (Billy Crystal)

How do you get holy water? You boil the hell out of it.

"Don't worry about avoiding temptation. As you grow older, it will avoid you." (Winston Churchill)

"Don't talk to me about Valentine's Day. At my age, an affair of the heart is a bypass."
(Joan Rivers)

I like the way your medication thinks.

I think they picked me for my motivational skills. Everyone always says they have to work twice as hard when I'm around.

If I had a dollar for every girl that found me unattractive, more girls would find me attractive.

Marriage is mostly misreading facial expressions and asking each other, "Are you okay?"

"Honesty may be the best policy, but it's important to remember that apparently, by elimination, dishonesty is the second-best policy." (George Carlin)

"I don't feel old. I don't feel anything until noon. Then it's time for my nap." (Bob Hope)

It's not hard to meet expenses... they're everywhere.

It's not the pace of life that concerns me, it's the sudden stop at the end.

No one is listening until you make a mistake.

All generalizations are false.

A little boy asked his father, "Daddy, how much does it cost to get married?" The father replied, "I don't know son, I'm still paying."

So what if I don't know what "Armageddon" means? It's not the end of the world.

I once took the 'p' out of a pirate. It made him very angry.

How do you know you're old? People call at 9 p.m. and ask, "Did I wake you?"

I asked my wife what she wanted for Christmas. She told me, "Nothing would make her happier than a diamond necklace." So, I bought her nothing.

I like to hold hands at the movies... which always seems to startle strangers.

What did one ocean say to the other ocean? Nothing, they just waved.

A girl said she recognized me from her vegetarian club, but I'd never met herbivore.

A woman worries about the future until she gets a husband. A man never worries about the future until he gets a wife.

A woman's mind is cleaner than a man's. She changes it more often.

I like to show my girlfriend who's boss in our house by holding a mirror up to her face.

What did the blanket say when it fell off the bed? "Oh sheet!"

What did the blonde say when she found out she was pregnant? "Are you sure it's mine?"

I'm feeling pretty proud of myself. The Sesame Street puzzle I bought said' 3-5 years', but I finished it in 18 months.

I like older men because they've gotten used to life's disappointments… which means they're ready for me.

What do you call cheese that isn't yours? Nacho cheese.

I told my wife that our kids were spoiled. She said, "No, they're not. All kids smell that way."

What do you call four bullfighters in quicksand? Quatro sinko.

I threw a boomerang a couple years ago; I now live in constant fear.

What do you call it when an Italian has one arm shorter than the other? A speech impediment.

What do you call Santa's helpers? Subordinate Clauses

I thought I was just really tired, but it's been 5 years, so I guess this is how I look now.

My memory has gotten so bad that it's actually caused me to lose my job. I'm still employed, I just can't remember where.

What do you call the saddest waterway in Russia? Crimea River.

I threw my toaster away because it kept burning my bread. You could say I'm black toast intolerant.

What do you call the security officers outside a Samsung Store? Guardians of the Galaxy.

What do you call the soft tissue between a shark's teeth? A slow swimmer.

I got caught in police speed trap yesterday. The officer walked up to my car and said, "I've been waiting all day for you." "Well," I said, "I got here as fast as I could."

My girlfriend and I often laugh about how competitive we are. But I laugh more.

If you're not supposed to eat at night, why is there a light bulb in the refrigerator?

What's blonde and dead and in a closet? The Hide and Seek Champion from 1995.

What's six inches long, two inches wide, and drives women wild? Money.

I'm reading a book about anti-gravity. It's impossible to put down.

My mind is made up. Don't confuse me with facts.

What's the best form of birth control after 50? Nudity

I tried to sue the airport for misplacing my luggage. I lost my case.

What's the difference between a girlfriend and a wife? 45 lbs.

I tried water polo, but my horse drowned.

What's the difference between a hippo and a zippo? One is really heavy and the other is a little lighter.

Outvoted 1-1 by my wife, again.

What's the difference between a poorly dressed man on a bicycle and a nicely dressed man on a tricycle? A tire.

I used to be able to do cartwheels. Now I tip over putting on my underwear.

My mind works like lightning. One brilliant flash, and it is gone.

What's the difference between baseball and politics? In baseball you're out if you're caught stealing.

If love is blind, why is lingerie so popular? (George Carlin)

What's the difference between men and pigs? Pigs don't turn into men when they drink.

If nothing was learned, nothing was taught.

What's the difference between a bad golfer and a bad skydiver? A bad golfer goes 'whack, damn;' a bad skydiver goes 'damn, whack.'

If number 666 is evil, then 25.8069758011 is the root of all evil.

If people could read my mind, I'd get punched in the face a lot.

My mom said that if I don't get off my computer and do my homework, she'll slam my head on the keyboard, but I think she's jokinfjreoiwjrtwe4to8rkljreun8f4ny84c8y4t58l.

What's the difference between a boyfriend and a husband? 45 minutes.

I got called 'pretty' today. Well, the full statement was 'you're pretty annoying,' but I try to focus on positive things.

There are so many scams on the Internet these days.... but for $19.95 I can show you how to avoid them.

There are three kinds of people: the ones who learn by reading; the ones who learn by observation; and the ones who have to touch the fire to learn it's hot.

I changed my password to "incorrect". So whenever I forget what it is the computer will say "Your password is incorrect".

Friendship is unnecessary ...like philosophy, like art. It has no survival value; rather, it is one of those things that gives value to survival.

My mother used to make me walk the plank when I was younger. We couldn't afford a dog.

I had a neck brace fitted years ago and I've never looked back since.

I had an hourglass figure, but then the sand shifted.

Why does it take 100 million sperms to fertilize one egg? Because they won't stop to ask directions.

My mother was so surprised when I told her I was born again. She said she didn't feel a thing!

How are a Texas tornado and a Tennessee divorce alike? Somebody's gonna to lose a trailer

Some men see marriage as an expensive way to
get laundry done for free.

You'll always stay young if you live honestly,
eat slowly, sleep sufficiently, work
industriously, worship faithfully, and lie
about your age.

Why do women have cleaner minds than
men? Because they change them more often.

I had amnesia once - maybe twice.

My father has schizophrenia, but he's good
people.

How do you catch a unique rabbit? Unique
up on it. How do you catch a tame rabbit?
Tame way. Unique up on it

What did one plate say to the other?
"Tonight, dinner's on me."

A teenager is God's punishment for enjoying
sex.

If you were to spell out numbers, how far
would you have to go to find the letter "A"?
One thousand

A termite walks into a bar and says, "Where is the bar tender?"

My email password has been hacked. That's the third time I've had to rename the cat.

My ex used to hit me with stringed instruments. If only I had known about her history of violins.

What do bulletproof vests, fire escapes, windshield wipers, and laser printers all have in common? They were all invented by women.

My first child has gone off to college and I feel a great emptiness in my life. Specifically, in my checking account.

My friend explained why he refuses to ever get married. He said that the wedding rings look too much like miniature handcuffs.

What do Eskimos get from sitting on the ice too long? Polaroids.

I have a fear of speed bumps, but I'm slowly getting over it.

I have a pencil that used to be owned by William Shakespeare, but he chewed it a lot. Now I can't tell if it's 2B or not 2B.

What do you call a Russian leader who's a procrastinator? Putinitoff

I don't think you act stupid, I'm sure it's the real thing.

If you yelled for 8 years, 7 months and 6 days, you would have produced enough sound energy to heat one cup of coffee.

So many people these days are so judgmental. I can tell just by looking at them.

My mother-in-law fell down a wishing well. I was amazed, I never knew they worked.

Why are so many blonde jokes one-liners? So brunettes can remember them.

My neighbors are listening to great music... whether they like it or not.

What do you call a tiny mother? A minimum.

You sound reasonable. It must be time to up my medication!

Your family tree must be a cactus because everybody on it is a prick.

What lies at the bottom of the ocean and twitches? A nervous wreck.

Men who have a pierced ear are better prepared for marriage. They've experienced pain and bought jewelry.

What differentiates "60 Minutes" on CBS from every other TV show? It has no theme song.

Never test the depth of the water with both feet.

Men read Playboy for the articles. Women go to malls for the music.

What should you do if you girlfriend starts smoking? Slow down and use a lubricant.

Behind every great man is a woman rolling her eyes.

Age is an issue of mind over matter. If you don't mind, it doesn't matter.

Scientists proved that cows don't give us meat and milk. We just take it from them.

What do you call an acid with an attitude? A mean-o-acid!

Behind every successful man, you'll find a woman who has nothing to wear.

I was addicted to the hokey pokey... but thankfully, I turned myself around.

Why couldn't the leopard play hide and seek? Because he was always spotted.

I was going to give him a nasty look, but he already had one.

Why do men find it difficult to make eye contact? Because breasts don't have eyes.

Recently, I've tried to make a car without wheels. I've been working on it tirelessly.

Red meat is not bad for you. Fuzzy green meat is bad for you.

Relationships are a lot like algebra. Have you ever looked at your X and wondered Y?

I wish conversations were like user agreements where you can skip to the end and just agree.

I went to the doctor today, and he refused to write me a prescription for Viagra. He said it would be like putting a new flagpole on a condemned building.

You know that tingly little feeling you get when you love someone? That's common sense leaving your body.

My therapist says I have a preoccupation with vengeance. We'll see about that!

I think my neighbor is stalking me. She's been Googling my name on her computer. I saw it through my telescope last night.

A courtroom artist was arrested today for an unknown reason. Details are sketchy.

Why do men want to marry virgins? They can't stand criticism.

A positive attitude may not solve all your problems, but it will annoy enough people to make it worth the effort.

A power struggle is an argument between two electric companies.

Did you hear about the kidnapping at school? It's okay. He woke up.

PMS jokes are not funny — period!

I wish the buck would stop here. I could use a few....

Did you hear there is a coin shortage in America? We're running out of common cents.

Polar bears are left-handed.

If you don't pay your exorcist, do you get repossessed?

Russian dolls are so full of themselves.

Politicians and diapers have one thing in common. They should both be changed regularly, and for the same reason.

I don't think you're stupid. You just have a bad luck when thinking.

If you don't like my opinion of you – improve yourself!

Why did God create alcohol? So ugly people could have sex, too.

Remember ...if the world didn't suck, we'd all fall off!

Scientist: "My findings are meaningless if taken out of context." Headline: Scientist claims: "Findings are meaningless."

I never thought I'd be the type of person to get up early in the morning to exercise. I was right.

A procrastinator's work is never done.

Why did the gym close? It just didn't work out!

I found there was only one way to look thin: hang out with fat people.

Seen it all. Done it all. Can't remember most of it.

Several guys are sitting around having a drink and one guy says, "My wife's an angel." Another guy says, "You're lucky. Mine's still alive."

Sex is like air; it's not important unless you aren't getting any.

A priest, a minister and a rabbit walk into a bar. The rabbit says, "I think I might be a typo."

On the keyboard of life, always keep one finger on the escape key.

Sometimes the only way you can feel good about yourself is by making someone else look bad. And I'm tired of making other people feel good about themselves!

On the other hand...you have different fingers.

Sex is like math. You add the bed, subtract the clothes, divide the legs, and pray that you don't multiply.

Silence is golden. Duct tape is silver.

Skeletons are always calm because nothing gets under their skin.

Small son sitting on Daddy's lap: "I'm still confused. Was I born in a nest or a hive?"

Apparently RSVP'ing back to a wedding invitation 'maybe next time' isn't the correct response.

Some days you're the bug... some days you're the windshield.

My teenage angst has lasted 30 years.

My wife said I never listen to her...or something like that.

I don't know what makes you so stupid, but it really works.

Why do we say something is out of whack? What's a whack?

If people from Poland are called Poles, why aren't people from Holland called Holes? (George Carlin)

Some days you're the dog, some days you're the hydrant.

A pig's orgasm lasts for 30 minutes. (In my next life I want to be a pig!)

Some lions mate over 50 times a day. (In my next life I still want to be a pig...quality over quantity!)

"In the school I went to, they asked a kid to prove the law of gravity and he threw the teacher out of the window." (Rodney Dangerfield)

If you find yourself in a hole, stop digging.

Sometimes someone unexpected comes into your life, makes your heart race, and changes you forever. We call those people 'the police'.

Don't be irreplaceable; if you can't be replaced, you can't be promoted.

She fell in love with a tennis player, but 'love' meant nothing to him.

She wanted a puppy. But I didn't want a puppy. So we compromised and got a puppy.

The last thing I want to do is hurt you; but it's still on the list.

If pro is the opposite of con, what is the opposite of progress?

Don't mess with old people. For them, life imprisonment is not that much of a deterrent anymore.

Sometimes, when I am matching socks, I think, "What if these two socks don't even like each other?"

Sorry I'm late. Traffic is exactly how it's been every day for the past 5 years, and I was not expecting that.

My wife likes it when I blow air on her when she's hot, but honestly... I'm not a fan.

If you get in the mood to do some work, someone will always wake you up.

Starfish do not have brains.

My daughter told me she wants to be a secret agent. Based on that alone, I don't think she'd be a good secret agent.

Strong people don't put others down. They lift them up and slam them on the ground for maximum damage.

Support bacteria - they're the only culture some people have.

Sure, I'd love to help you out. Which way did you come in?

Sweet dreams are made of cheese. Who am I to dis a brie?

Take my advice — I'm not using it.

Talk is cheap because supply exceeds demand.

Taxes are the price we pay for a civilization. In light of recent results, I want my money back.

If shit was music, you'd be an orchestra.

Tell me again how I unloaded the dishwasher too loudly when you were watching golf. Detectives will want to know exactly how this went down.

My wife says I only have two faults — I don't listen...and something else.

What's the difference between a kleptomaniac and a literalist? A literalist takes things literally and a kleptomaniac takes things, literally.

If Fed Ex and UPS were to merge, would they call it Fed Up?

Tell me to 'Stuff it!'. I'm a taxidermist.

If a pig loses its voice, is it disgruntled?

Tell me what you need, and I'll tell you how to get along without it.

Thanks once again to autocorrect, my sister's kids are expecting the Easter Rabbi tomorrow.

The 50-50-90 Rule: Anytime you have a 50-50 chance of getting something right, there's a 90% probability you'll get it wrong.

The average number of people airborne over the US any given hour is 61,000.

My husband and I were happy for 20 years. And then we met.

If a parsley farmer gets sued and loses, can they garnish his wages?

I'm Pining for a good tree pun. I wish they were more Poplar.

Why do we drive on a parkway and park on a driveway?

The last person that quit or was fired will be held responsible or everything that goes wrong.

If procrastination were an Olympic sport, I'd compete in it later.

The average woman would rather have beauty than brains, because the average man can see better than he can think.

The best way to a man's heart is to saw his breast plate open.

The book on chronology I ordered has finally arrived. It's about time...

I lost 150 pounds in one day. I got divorced.

If you glue a dead wasp to your palm, you can smack your boss on the back of the head as hard as you want and act like you saved him.

If you keep your feet firmly on the ground, you'll have trouble putting on your pants.

The cardiologist's diet: If it tastes good, spit it out.

My wife and I have reached the difficult decision that we do not want children. If anybody does, please just send me your contact information, and we can drop them off.

I refused to believe my father, the road worker, was stealing from his job, but when I got home all the signs were there.

I relish the fact that you've mustard the strength to ketchup to me.

I remember being in so much debt that I couldn't afford my electricity bills. It was a dark time.

The catfish has over 27,000 taste buds, that makes the catfish rank #1 for animal having the most taste buds.

The depressing thing about tennis is that no matter how good I get, I'll never be as good as a wall.

The difference between an oral thermometer and a rectal thermometer is in the taste.

I asked my husband if he remembers what today is... Scaring men is easy.

Why is a person who plays the piano called a 'pianist', but a person who drives a race car is not called a 'racist?'

The flea can jump 350 times its body length. It's like a human jumping the length of a football field.

The human heart creates enough pressure when it pumps out to the body to squirt blood 30 feet.

I buy all my guns from a guy called T-Rex.
He's a small arms dealer.

I like you. You remind me of when I was
young and stupid.

The journey of a thousand miles begins with
a broken fan belt and a leaky tire.

Love is telling someone to go to hell and
worrying about them getting there safely.

The last airline I flew on charged for
everything—except for the bad service. That
was free.

The lesson of Halloween is that pretending to
be something you're not will lead to a sweet
reward.

Why is a bra singular and panties plural?

I once worked as a salesman and was very
independent. I took orders from no one.

The look in my wife's eyes when she left for
Target makes me think she is going to try and
save the economy in one trip.

The man who created autocorrect has died.
Restaurant in peace.

The man who invented knock-knock jokes should get a no bell prize.

Moses had the first tablet that could connect to the cloud.

When the cannibal showed up late to the buffet, they gave him the cold shoulder.

What language are you speaking? Because it sounds like bullshit.

What makes men chase women they have no intention of marrying them? The same urge that makes dogs chase cars they have no intention of driving.

The man who survived both mustard gas and pepper spray is a seasoned veteran now.

The more crap you put up with, the more crap you are going to get.

The more people I meet, the more I like my dog.

He who laughs last thinks slowest.

He: "I started seeing someone. She: "As in dating or hallucinations?"

What kind of coffee was served on the Titanic? Sanka

He: "Personally, bad English is such a turn-off for me." She: "You don't need 'for me' after saying 'personally'."

When the chips are down, the buffalo is empty.

Last night I played a blank tape at full blast. The mime next door went nuts.

The most effective way to remember your wife's birthday is to forget it once.

The names of all the continents end with the same letter that they start with.

The nice part about living in a small town is that when you don't know what you're doing, someone else does.

The officer said, "You drinking?" I said, "You buying?" We just laughed and laughed.... I need bail money.

It takes patience to listen. It takes skill to pretend you're listening.

It used to be only death and taxes were inevitable. Now, of course, there's shipping and handling, too.

It was an emotional wedding. Even the cake was in tiers.

Why do they put pictures of criminals up in the Post Office? What are we supposed to do, write to them? Why don't they just put their pictures on the postage stamps so the mailmen can look for them while they deliver the mail?

The older I get, the earlier it gets late.

The only difference between a rut and a grave is the depth.

The only time the world beats a path to your door is when you're in the bathroom.

The only two days of the year in which there are no professional sports games in the MLB, NBA, NHL, or NFL are the day before and the day after the MLB League All-Star Game.

The people who go to conferences are the ones who shouldn't.

The price of gas is so high that the mailman is working from home. He called me yesterday to read me my bills.

The problem with kleptomaniacs is that they always take things... literally.

The problem with political jokes is that sometimes they get elected.

The quickest way to double your money is to fold it in half and put it back in your pocket.

The reason Mayberry was so peaceful and quiet was because nobody was married. Andy, Aunt Bea, Barney, Floyd, Howard, Goober, Gomer, Sam, Earnest T Bass, Helen, Thelma Lou, Clara and, of course, Opie were all single. The only married person was Otis, and he was a drunk.

If you can't laugh at yourself, let me do it.

If you cross an owl and a rooster, do you get a cock that stays up all night?

Why do 'overlook' and 'oversee' mean opposite things?

"Diapers and politicians should be changed often...and for the same reason." (Mark Twain)

The reason most people play golf is to wear clothes they wouldn't otherwise be caught dead in.

The reason that a dog has so many friends is that he wags his tail instead of his tongue.

The reward for a job well done is more work.

The right to be heard does not automatically include the right to be taken seriously.

The rotation of Earth really makes my day.

The San Francisco Cable cars are the only mobile National Monuments.

Confucius teaches that we should love one another. If that doesn't work, just reverse the last two words.

If you're not supposed to eat at night, why is there a light bulb in the refrigerator?

There's nothing like the joy on a kid's face when he first sees the PlayStation box containing the socks I got him for Christmas.

The shortest book in the world *What Men Know About Women.*

Why do croutons come in airtight packages? Aren't they just stale bread to begin with?

The statistics on sanity are that one out of every four Americans is suffering from some form of mental illness. Think of your three best friends. If they're okay, then it's you.

The sun is going to go out in 4 billion years, and you sit there and act like everything is fine.

The teacher said that that 'that' that that girl used in a sentence was correct.

My wife and I always compromise. I admit I'm wrong and she agrees with me.

What is the difference between a dog and a fox? About 5 drinks.

The strongest muscle in the body is the tongue.

Children: You spend the first 2 years of their life teaching them to walk and talk. Then you spend the next 16 years telling them to sit down and shut up.

Cleaning mirrors is a job I could really see myself doing.

Hard work has a future payoff. Laziness pays off now.

The trouble with work is … it's so daily.

If you can't say something nice, say it to your husband. He's not listening anyway.

I worked in the woods as a lumberjack, but I just couldn't hack it, so they gave me the ax.

The word 'listen' contains the same letters as the word 'silent'.

The word racecar and kayak are the same whether they are read left to right or right to left.

The world champion tongue twister got arrested. I hear they're going to give him a tough sentence.

The world's youngest parents were 8 and 9 and lived in China in 1910.

He always finds himself lost in thought; it's unfamiliar territory.

He doesn't know the meaning of fear... but then again, he doesn't know the meaning of most words.

I thought about how American mothers feed their babies with tiny little spoons and forks and I wondered if Chinese mothers use toothpicks.

I thought growing old would take longer.

The youngest pope was 11 years old.

I worked myself up from nothing to a state of extreme poverty.

Therapist: "Your wife says you never buy her flowers. Is that true?" Me: "To be honest, I never knew she sold flowers."

There are 12 things people do when they haven't prepared a speech. They lie, tell stories, and exaggerate.

A crocodile cannot stick its tongue out.

Why do bees hum? They don't remember the lyrics.

There may be no excuse for laziness, but I'm still looking.

There's never enough time to do it right, but there's always enough time to do it over.

There's no 'I' in team, but there is a 'U' in suck.

There's nothing I've learned from being a father that I couldn't just as easily have figured out from setting all my money on fire.

Experience is something you don't get until just after you need it.

There's a fine line between numerator and denominator. (Only a fraction of people will find that funny.)

They keep saying the right person will come along. I think mine got hit by a truck.

Last night in my dream I was peeing in bed. In the morning I realized that dreams do come true.

They say you are what you eat, so lay off nuts.

On average people fear spiders more than they do death.

Think of how stupid the average person is and realize half of them are more stupid than that.

This morning some clown opened the door for me. I thought to myself, 'That's a nice Jester.'

Those of you who think you know it all are really annoying to those of us who do!

Three of my favorite things are eating my family and not using commas.

A book fell on my head the other day. I only have my shelf to blame.

What is Forest Gump's password? 1Forest1.

What's the latest possible date that I can still make something of my life?

Tim bought 2 goldfish and named them '1' and '2'. That way, if '1' died, he'll still have '2'.

Time is the best teacher. Unfortunately, it kills all of its students.

Time is what keeps everything from happening at once.

Time may be a great healer but it's also a lousy beautician.

I am now on three dating sites because you can never get enough rejection.

Why can't women read maps? Only the male mind can comprehend the concept of one inch equaling a mile.

To err is human; to forgive is not our policy.

To leave a party without telling anyone is called in English, a "French Exit". In French, it's called a "partir a l'anglaise", to leave like the English.

To me, drinking responsibly means not spiling any.

A man knocked on my door and asked for a small donation toward the local swimming pool. I gave him a glass of water.

Today was a terrible day. My ex got hit by a bus, and I lost my job as a bus driver.

Today, my son asked, "Can I have a bookmark?" and I burst into tears. 11 years old and he still doesn't know my name is Brian.

Old teacher: "If I say, 'I am beautiful,' which tense is that?" Young student: "It's obviously past."

One of the cows didn't produce milk today. It was an udder failure.

What if soy milk is just regular milk introducing itself in Spanish?

What if there were no hypothetical questions?

With great reflexes comes great response ability.

Tomorrow is a big day for me at work. They are refilling the snack vending machine.

Top 3 situations that require witnesses: 1) Crimes 2) Accidents 3) Marriages. Need I say more?

Twitter is great if you can't afford therapy, and you also don't want to get any better.

What do you call a man with a rubber toe? Roberto.

Two cheese trucks ran into each other. De brie was everywhere.

Two Wi-Fi engineers got married. The reception was fantastic.

Two wrongs don't make a right; take your parents for example....

TYPEWRITER is the longest word that can be made using the letters on only one row of the keyboard.

Under my gruff exterior lies an even gruffer interior.

What do you call a meditating wolf? Aware wolf.

What do you call a monkey that loves Doritos? A chipmonk.

Two artists had an art contest. It ended in a draw.

What do you call a row of rabbits hopping away? A receding hare line.

Unless you're the lead dog, the view never changes.

Veni, Vedi, Visa: I came, I saw, I did a little shopping.

Very funny, Scotty. Now beam down my clothes.

Want to hear my opinion, or should I go to hell again?

We all sprang from apes, but you didn't spring far enough.

Welcome to Utah: set your watch back 20 years.

"I failed math so many times at school, I can't even count." (Stewart Francis)

"I had a rose named after me and I was very flattered. But I was not pleased to read the description in the catalogue: - 'No good in a bed, but fine against a wall.'" (Eleanor Roosevelt)

What a lovely surprise to finally discover how unlonely being alone can be.

What do you call a sad cup of coffee? A depresso.

Rest in peace boiling water. You will be mist.

I saw a sign that said, 'Watch for children' and I thought, 'That sounds like a fair trade.'

What do you call a cat that likes to eat beans? Puss 'n' Toots.

I get plenty of exercise - jumping to conclusions, pushing my luck, and dodging deadlines.

I got a case for my iPhone even though the screen was already cracked. Basically, it's like putting a condom on my kid's head.

"The New England Journal of Medicine reports that 9 out of 10 doctors agree that 1 out of 10 doctors is an idiot." (Jay Leno)

"The secret of a good sermon is to have a good beginning and a good ending— and to have the two as close together as possible." (George Burns)

What do you call a witch who lives at the beach? A sand-witch.

What do you call an elephant that doesn't matter? An irrelephant.

What do you call cheese that doesn't belong to you? Nacho cheese.

What do you call it when a cat wins a dog show? A cat-has-trophy.

What do you call it when one cow spies on another? A steak out.

What do you call the wife of a hippie?
Mississippi.

What do you call twin dinosaurs? A pair-
odactyls.

So, a thought crossed your mind? It must
have been a long and lonely journey.

Drink wine. It isn't good to keep things
bottled up.

Whatever happened to Preparations A
through G?

When my boss asked me who was stupid, me
or him, I told him he doesn't hire stupid
people.

Whiteboards are remarkable.

Who stopped payment on my reality check?

Whoever said nothing is impossible is a liar.
I've been doing nothing for years.

Why are a 'wise man' and a 'wise guy'
opposites?

When a woman says "What?" it's not because she didn't hear you. She's just giving you a chance to change what you said.

Don't be sad when a bird craps on your head. Be happy that dogs can't fly.

Don't let your worries get the best of you. Remember: Moses started out as a basket case.

Don't marry for money; you can borrow it cheaper.

What do you call an avocado that's been blessed? Holy Guacamole.

Don't trust atoms. They make up everything.

Why is "you're a peach" a complement but "you're bananas" an insult? Why are we allowing fruit discrimination to tear society apart?

Why is abbreviated is such a long word?

What do you call a blonde with half a brain? Gifted.

Christmas - What other time of the year do you sit in front of a dead tree and eat candy out of your socks?

Why is the day that you do laundry, cook, clean, iron and so on, called a day off?

My Wi-Fi went down for five minutes, so I had to talk to my family. They seem like nice people.

Wise people think all they say. Fools say all they think.

With great power comes a great electricity bill. Watt a powerful message.

Yesterday I donated my watch, phone, and $500 to a poor guy. You can't imagine the happiness I felt as I saw him put his pistol back in his pocket.

You are about to exceed the limits of my medication.

Why I love Spanish:

I. Mi pap6 tiene 47 acos. (My dad is 47 years old.) 2. Mi papa tiene 47 anos. (My potato has 47 assholes.)

About the Editor

A former city and property manager, college professor, and judge, Andrew Felder is a part-time attorney and full-time editor and publisher of The Network Magazine. The author of several books, he has tackled a wide variety of subject matter including humor, psychology, and romance. A native New Yorker, and the father of three and grandfather of seven, he currently lives in Fort Worth with his wife, Bette, and Aussiedoodle, Annabelle.

Also available from Andrew A. Felder